11/15/2016

DAWN,

I hope you enjoy
read my book Unshackled
as much as I enjoyed livi

it.

GOD IS FAITHFUL

GENE

ENDORSEMENTS

"I'm pleased to recommend *Unshackled* to you. Gene's is a powerful testimony of how our God's love pursues, how His mercy heals, and how His grace translates ruins to redemption. It's the story of a man set free! And he whom the Son sets free ... is free indeed!" –Greg Laurie, Pastor, Harvest Christian Fellowship, Evangelist, Harvest Crusades

"Perhaps nobody understands or appreciates freedom as much as Gene McGuire—not because he was locked up for almost 35 years, but because he experienced the freedom that only Christ can bring, even while still behind bars. Now that he has been released from prison, he is able to share the truths that enable all of us to experience greater emotional and spiritual freedom." –James Robison, Founder of LIFE Outreach International

"Gene's story is a powerful example of the hope of Christ that can penetrate the darkest of situations. Sentenced to life in prison at the age of 17 for being in the wrong place at the wrong time, life couldn't get much worse for Gene. Yet I was encouraged by how God's love found him in the midst of such tragic circumstances. Gene's story is impactful for all of us because if God could bring hope to one man in such trying circumstances, then God can surely do it for us, no matter how difficult a situation we find ourselves in. Gene shows us that no matter what we face, we can give thanks in all circumstances just as Paul wrote to believers in 1 Thessalonians 5:16-18, 'Rejoice always, pray continually, give thanks in all circumstances; for this is God's will for you in Christ Jesus.'" –Dr. Kyle Lance Martin, Time to Revive

"My life was changed when I posed for a picture with one of the most mystical examples of the miraculous of my lifetime. I stood with Dr. Nelson Mandela who, two months before, was released from over 20 years of imprisonment for leading the fight for justice and freedom in South Africa. The most amazing thing about this man was his unbelievable sense of peace, humility and unimaginable spirit of forgiveness. I could not imagine a victim of injustice whose life had been shackled and left in shambles and come out with no bitterness. Something in me concluded that no man could go through such a prolonged ordeal and emerge with a godly humble spirit... that is, until I met Gene McGuire! You will read this work with continued exclamations of 'unbelievable,' 'how could he?' and 'I don't believe it.' You will experience the healing power of the Christ, Lord of Gene's life. Gene McGuire's book adds a new dimension to the clarion testimony of deliverance, 'Free at last; free at last; thank God Almighty, I'm free at last.'" –Bishop Kenneth C. Ulmer, DMin, PhD, Faithful Central Bible Church, Los Angeles, CA

"Gene McGuire's story is truly inspirational and faith-affirming. It's a testimony of God's amazing grace and the power of His love to transform a life. Gene didn't find a religion in prison, he found Jesus, and Jesus changed everything for him. It's a powerful story of truth and consequences; forgiveness, faithfulness, fortitude and freedom." –Pastor Larry Huch, Founder and Senior Pastor, DFW New Beginnings, Bedford, TX

"Riveting, captivating and compelling—the authentic life of Gene McGuire. *Unshackled* is far more than just the heart-wrenching story of a man who served 35 years in prison for another man's crime. It is a testimony of God's grace coupled with discipleship 101 to 401. Read it and be impacted." –Larry Titus, President, Kingdom Global Ministries

"I am proud to know Gene as a friend, mentor and brother. He's a man of God whose faithfulness, integrity and character still shines brightly in the dark halls of SCI Rockview. *Unshackled* is a testament of God's enduring grace and boundless love at work in those who serve Him. Philippians 4:9." –Henry Smolarski, fellow life-sentenced inmate and disciple

"Gene McGuire's story is riveting. It will strike the reader on many different levels. It will especially encourage those who feel trapped by life's circumstances, or who think God's process of transformation is moving too slow. I met Gene several years ago and corresponded with him while he was in prison. In all his letters he assured me of his prayers for us and our ministry. Gene is a man filled with the Holy Spirit. He has a powerful message for all who will hear it." –Valson Abraham, Founder of India Gospel Outreach,

President, India Bible College & Seminary

"This book should be required reading for every man or women who ministers to the incarcerated. Gene reached deep into his memory to share the feelings that those who have never been in prison need to understand and the hope that each inmate needs to successfully transition to a life in Jesus. For almost 25 years I was touched by his life through the letters we exchanged. Gene's truly *Unshackled* life inspires me. It's one of the main reasons I got into prison ministry. I will be giving his book to the men I work with and those I write to. I know it will reach them on a level that I can't and for that I am truly grateful!" –Stephen Sands, Founder and Co-Director of Friends Over Fences

"Gene McGuire's story is truly life changing! I watched firsthand how Gene's testimony impacted our entire cogeneration! *Unshackled* will inspire people of all ages! Gene is eminently qualified to guide people on the pathway to a true relationship with Christ." –Shane Wilson, Lead Pastor, Christian Life Assembly, Camp Hill, PA

"When Gene speaks to our employees about his time in prison a dramatic hush falls over the room. His testimony revealed in this book shows God's hand, freeing him from a life sentence with no chance of freedom. His powerful story compels others to recognize the tragedy in their own lives and permits them to move beyond their own past."—Paul Vinyard, Owner, Babe's Chicken Dinner House, Bubba's Cooks Country, Sweetie Pie's Ribeyes

"It is an honor for me to endorse Gene McGuire's book, *Unshackled*. More importantly, I endorse how Gene is living out his life. This book exemplifies a life changed by the power of God. You will be encouraged as you see God's love at work in all situations. Gene's life is a testimony that *'all things work together for the glory of God.'*" –Tillie Burgin, Executive Director, Mission Arlington/Mission Metroplex

"The Bible says, 'For we are God's handiwork, created in Christ Jesus to do good works, which God prepared in advance for us to do.' *Unshackled:*

From Ruin to Redemption reveals God's handiwork in the life and person of Gene McGuire, prison lifer to lifelong ambassador of the Gospel, and one of the best friends God has ever given me. This book is a tears to triumph story of God's faithfulness and grace. You'll pick it up and be unable to put it down." –Ricky Griffin, Pastor, Trinity Fellowship Association of Churches

UNSHACKLED

FROM RUIN TO
REDEMPTION

BY

GENE McGUIRE

WITH DARIN MICHAEL SHAW

21 20 19 18 17   10 9 8 7 6 5 4 3 2 1

UNSHACKLED: From Ruin to Redemption

Published by:
Emerge Publishing, llc
9521B Riverside Parkway Suite 243
Tulsa, Oklahoma 74137
Phone 888.407.4447
www.EmergePublishing.com

Library of Congress Cataloging-in-Publication Data
McGuire, Eugene

ISBN: 978-1-943127-43-6 Hardcover
ISBN: 978-1-943127-44-3 Digital/E-book

BISAC Category:
REL012040 RELIGION / Christian Life / Inspirational
BIO024000 BIOGRAPHY & AUTOBIOGRAPHY / Criminals & Outlaws

Printed in the United States of America

FOREWORD

One of the most amazing privileges of traveling with Harvest Crusades is meeting people and hearing their stories—each a piece of God's larger, unfolding redemptive story.

Cathe and I met Gene McGuire while the Harvest team was in Dallas. We were introduced and told he had an amazing testimony—Gene was sentenced to life in prison without the possibility of parole, and spent 35 years there ... for a murder he didn't commit.

In an impromptu setting, Gene shared his story with us.

A broken home, dysfunctional family, alcoholism, teen rebellion—its start was typical of many stories you'd hear. Convicted of murder at 17 ... now that's something you don't hear every day!

A woman died. The lives of many others—family, friends, members of the tight-knit, small town community—were forever changed. But, as is always the case with our God, tragedy wouldn't have the last word.

Gene's story takes you from that fateful night, the scene of the crime, through years of running from God, to a place where he finally fell on his knees before Him—and the amazing transformation it brought about in his heart and life.

As Gene shared his story, Cathe and I were amazed to realize that even after 35 years in prison for a murder he didn't commit, Gene is at peace! He's not shackled to guilt, shame, or bitterness. He's forgiven those involved and the system that failed him. He truly is *Unshackled!*

Gene's is a powerful testimony of how our God's love pursues, how His mercy heals, and how His grace translates ruins to redemption. It can be your testimony, too.

I'm pleased to recommend *Unshackled* to you. It's the story of a man set free! And he whom the Son sets free ... is free indeed!

Greg Laurie, Pastor, Harvest Christian Fellowship
Evangelist, Harvest Crusades

ACKNOWLEDGEMENT

"Unless a grain of wheat falls into the earth and dies, it remains alone; but if it dies, it bears much fruit." –John 12:24

An investor is someone who provides a resource for an enterprise, expecting a gain or return for their sacrifice. The following people have been Investors in my life, sacrificing their resources in order to experience both an eternal gain and a greater level of fruitfulness on earth.

Pastors Larry & Devi Titus, Kingdom Global Ministries

Paul Vinyard, Joel Vinyard & Tiffany Vinyard Wheeless
Owners of Babes Chicken Dinner House

Bill & Karen Nast, Grace & Glory Outreach

J. David Ford, President at J David Ford & Associates, Inc.

Thomas A. Reitz, Chaplain SCI Rockview

Jim Neary & Cindy McCarty of the Wyoming County Probation Office

Darin Michael Shaw, Writer

My family, Joe & Mary Yuhas, Stephanie and Mark

I thank God for you all!

PREFACE

They're like pictures on the walls of my mind. The little lake. The narrow lake road. A small dirt parking lot. The old Marine Room Tavern. Memories flashed through my mind as we approached—incredibly vivid—even though 38 years had passed. It seemed as if it was only yesterday.

Things happened so fast on that night long ago. I didn't think about any of it—just acted in the moment. Now I'd returned, having had nearly four decades to replay those scenes in my mind and wonder "What if?" and "If only..." over and over again.

I had a strange sense that this was the right timing for me to revisit the scene. For years I'd wanted to walk back into the tavern—maybe to bring closure, I don't know, maybe to mentally settle all that had taken place there that night. My mind sometimes played tricks on me—*Had this really happened? Was it all a very bad dream?* Standing there, looking at the door, it was very real.

As I prepared to walk inside, I felt a weight, a tightness, develop within my chest. For a moment I even tried to talk myself out of stepping inside, thinking, *Maybe I don't belong here. Maybe those inside wouldn't want me here. If anyone saw me and remembered me—put two and two together—'Hey, you're that guy!'—I don't deserve to be here.*

The front of the tavern looked almost exactly as I remember it. The bright afternoon sun revealed the building's neglect—the blue siding had all faded, pieces of black tar-paper were visible where portions of siding had rotted or been broken away. I hadn't been inside that place since I was 17—a sophomore in high school.

The only way to describe the experience? It felt like I was walking through a dark tunnel into my past. I was retracing the steps I, my cousin Bobby, and my step-brother, Sid, had taken that hot June evening in 1977.

I paused for a moment at the exact spot in the parking lot where I'd stood before, about 20 yards from the door. An old automotive oil stain marked the location. My friend Darin, who has helped me tell my story, was with me. He noticed my hesitation and asked, "Are you okay?"

"Yeah," I said. "Just remembering."

I began to speak my thoughts: "We were so drunk that night. None of us were thinking straight. We were just following Bobby. Whatever idea he had seemed like a good one. I can still recall the conversations." Indeed, every word, every step, every happening of that infamous night flashed, now, as intense scenes in my mind. I don't recall if I spoke out loud or just thought: "I can't believe I'm here."

"You up for going inside?" Darin asked.

Still apprehensive, I put one foot in front of the other toward the door. I felt like I was walking on sacred ground. What had taken place here so many years ago—all in a matter of just a few moments—had changed the course of many lives. I've had to own that. And I have. But it was all coming back.

Just opening the door, stepping through it, brought a rush of emotion. It also gave a tangible and haunting context to my recollections—the darkness, the music in the background, the smell of stale beer and cigarette smoke, a few "regulars" at the bar—it was as if I'd gone back in time.

I studied the 15-foot-long bar and the barstools that ran its length. I looked briefly to the left—where it all happened—the darkest corner of the bar. I had to look away.

Some nice folks, sitting and sipping their beers, noticed us walk in. I smiled their direction and immediately began to worry. *Did they recognize me?*

A couple years earlier, I'd been in town to tell my story at a few local churches. On the way to my sister's house from the airport, I stopped into a salon for a quick haircut. I was chatting with the lady trimming my hair when her co-worker spun around, pointed at me with the scissors in her hand, and said, "You're him, aren't you?"

My heart just about stopped! I felt all the blood rush out of my face. Then she continued, "You're the guy in the newspaper article, speaking at the church in Clark's Green on Sunday, aren't you?"

"Yes, this Sunday. Clark's Green," I said, able to breathe again. "I just flew in from Dallas."

"You're Mary's brother," my hair stylist contributed. "Mary from Mill City?"

"Everybody knows Mary," said the scissor-pointing lady. "She's the nicest person in town!"

I sighed in relief. "Yes, I'm Mary's brother."

It was that same sort of fear that gripped me as I stood in the bar. What if someone said something? "Are you that guy?..."

I wondered if the lady behind the bar was the current owner. She looked too young to be an owner. Isabelle Nagy had been 60. This lady looked only to have been in her 30s. Did she know the story of what had happened here long ago? I began wrestling—*Should I just leave? Should I sit down and stay a little while? What was the right thing to do?*

I had to make a decision. I couldn't very well just stand there in front of the bar looking around.

Darin called out to the bartender, "Could we get a couple Cokes?" Decision made. He kicked a stool out in front of me, "Grab a seat."

We sat for several moments. I tried to take it all in. I looked up at the tavern's cigarette smoke-stained lighting. It hadn't been updated in decades—probably the very same lights that hung there that night. I looked back at the bar. It seemed a little shorter to me, maybe resurfaced over the years. A few things behind the bar may have been rearranged, but not much. For the most part, everything looked very similar to my own memory of it.

As I've said, scenes flashed—I'd remember this sight, then that one. Everywhere I looked, an image would materialize, then just as quickly fade—like watching a slideshow. I was reliving the whole event—walking through that night step-by-step in my mind. I had to stop. I tried to come back to the here and now.

I started to speak to my friend, but quietly so no one else would realize why we were there. "That counter over there is different. The pizza oven and those hanging lights are the same."

I stepped away from the bar and walked toward the pool table. He followed. "This pool table and the Coors lamp hanging over it—they were here that night. Everything is exactly the same."

I retraced the steps Bobby, Sid, and me took; we walked around this table. I looked to the bar. I remembered where Isabelle had been standing. I saw where our two Cokes were sitting on the bar now—just about where we'd picked up our shots and beers 38 years ago.

"What else do you remember?" my friend asked.

"Pool," I said, taking the cue ball in hand and rolling it down the length of the table. "And losing! I'd used my cousin's ID to get served, and was so inebriated that I could hardly hit the ball straight. I could hardly see straight."

My cousin Bobby was good with a pool cue, even drunk as he was. I remember him looking at me and smiling with each of my failed shots. But just a little while of playing pool and then everything changed. I didn't want to go there. I tried to shift my mind, and our dialogue, to something else.

"Those tables and chairs, they're the same," I said, now bouncing the cue ball off the cushion. "And that cigarette machine over there—it's in the same position it was on that night." It was as if I'd traveled back in time. Very unsettling.

"Had enough?" Darin asked.

"Yeah," I replied. He paid for our Cokes, and we stepped back out into the bright sun.

Next we drove to the courthouse—the courthouse where I'd been convicted in 1977 and released in 2012. I'd made a dozen or so trips back to the courthouse these last few years. I have a number of friends there.

With every trip back to Pennsylvania, I like to stop in and update everyone on my life—and thank them again. But in all those trips, I'd never met nor spoken to the judge who set me free. I wanted to see him, to shake his hand, to thank him. I wanted to look him in the eye and assure him that he would never regret his decision to release me. But you just don't get appointments to see judges.

This trip, I was taking my friend to meet the probation and parole staff who had been instrumental in my case, a few of the officers there who had been so kind and supportive to me, and to sit in the courtroom itself—the very chair where I'd not only heard my sentence—"the rest of your natural life"—but in which I was also, 34 years, nine months, and 15 days later, released.

As we were wrapping up our visit and waiting for an elevator, the door opened and a shorter white-haired gentleman, wearing a well-pressed white shirt and dark suspenders, stepped out. I was finally face-to-face with the man.

Someone introduced us: "Gene, this is Judge Shurtleff."

I didn't recognize him from three years earlier. He seemed so much bigger to me then, up at the bench, sitting in a big leather chair, cloaked in black robes, gavel in hand. I reached out my hand to bridge the space between us, the expressionless look on his face made it difficult to form the words, but form them I did. "Hi. I'm Gene McGuire."

He remained silent. I continued: "I want to say thank you very much for all you and your staff did for me. I really appreciate all you've done."

It may have only been a second, but it felt like an eternity—he just looked at me. My mind started spinning. Emotions welled up. *Did he have regrets? Had he had second thoughts about releasing me?* My heart sank.

"Gene McGuire," Judge Shurtleff finally spoke.

This was really an answer to prayer. I'd longed for this moment—and to think, had we taken the stairs or arrived at the elevator a moment earlier or later, it wouldn't have happened.

"I think about you every time I pass by that prison up there when visiting a relative of mine at Penn State. I think ... you're probably the only lifer I'll ever release."

There was a pregnant pause. I stood trying to interpret his words—did he think he'd made a mistake? Then he continued...

"But it was absolutely the right thing to do." And he shook my hand.

"Are you still with the folks in Dallas?" he asked. "Yes, sir, your Honor. I am working as a pastor for a large Christian and family-owned restaurant. I serve the staff in numerous locations. I love it."

"Very good."

He never smiled, but his eyes showed approval. And then, just as quickly as he'd appeared before us, he was gone. I looked at my friend Darin in disbelief that this encounter had just taken place.

He asked me, "You okay?"

I nodded. "Yes. Yes, I am okay."

I went back—back to the scene, back to the courthouse—because so much of my story unfolded there.

And it's my privilege, in this book, to share my story with you. To take you back and to walk you through those scenes—the sights, sounds, events—to walk you through the first 17 years of my life, and then the next 35; through the most tragic of all my decisions and actions and the most beneficial and life-changing; through the deep, deep darkness and into the magnificent and resplendent light.

Thank you for coming with me.

AK4192

CHAPTER 1

IT'S ALL
A LITTLE HAZY

Sid and I stood frozen in the doorway. Neither of us said a word.

Bobby rose up behind the bar; there was blood all over his shirt, face, and hands. He caught a glimpse of us and yelled, "Don't just stand there! Help me find the money!"

He turned his attention to the cash register on the bar. "There's got to be more than this," he said, gathering and taking inventory of the small bills in the till. He stepped back over to where she lay, pulling at her clothing—hoping, I suppose, to reveal a money belt or to find some cash in her pockets.

The next thing I knew, I had stepped into the dining area and was rummaging for anything of value. I was drunk. We all were. Alcohol, adrenaline, and fear—it's all pretty hazy. I remember the jukebox on one wall, and the cigarette machine in the back of the room. I poked around at them for a minute or two, and must have looked for something I could use to pry open the change boxes.

Bobby went to the sink behind the bar. He started washing her blood off of his hands—some of his own, too, as he had cut himself during the attack. "Come over here," he called. I joined him, searching behind the bar and through a passage into the kitchen—it was dark, hard to see. We didn't find anything of value.

"Let's look around back," Bobby said. We went out the door, down around and behind the building. There were some storage areas there, a shed or two. We were in and out, in and out—again, so dark, we couldn't see anything.

We found nothing. When we'd exhausted all options outside, I followed him back to the front.

"The damn door is locked!" Bobby said. It must have locked behind us when we came out. He busted a window next to the front door with his elbow, and I crawled through it. Inside, I climbed over a red leather bench that sat beneath the window, popped up, and unlocked the door to let Bobby back in.

"There's gotta be more money!" he shouted. He headed back behind the bar to search a second time.

Curiosity drew me to my left, toward the pizza counter. *What exactly had happened? Was she really dead? What did a dead woman look like?* I took a few nervous steps and then leaned over the counter to see. There she was, in the shadows, motionless. There was a lot of blood. I couldn't really see much detail. I tried to put it in perspective—her life was over and mine would never be the same again. Bobby stooped down next to her body, looked up at me, and said, "I didn't mean to kill her, Gene." I don't really remember, but I don't think I said a word.

"There!" he said, spying a small metal cashbox on a shelf under the bar, right above her body. The box had a flimsy lock. In an instant, Bobby had pried it open with his bare hands, revealing a stack of cash inside. "It must be about a thousand bucks!" Beneath the cash, there were several sleeves of mint coins—a coin collection. Bobby began tucking the money into his pockets, instructing, "We've gotta get out of here!"

It hadn't dawned on either of us yet—Sid was gone. "Where the hell is Sid?"

"Shhh...! He took the car and left!" Bobby was certain Sid would tell on us. We noticed the lady's maroon Oldsmobile Cutlass parked right outside the door. Bobby dashed behind the bar again, this time fishing through her purse to find the keys. We drove away in her car.

It was only a few miles back to my house. I can't recall saying a word. My mind was going a hundred miles a minute, but I only remember Bobby talking. "I didn't mean to kill her. I mean ... I wasn't planning on it. I was only going to rob her. I said, 'This is a robbery.' She threw an ashtray at me. Hit me in the head. I lost it, Gene. Why didn't she just give me the damn money?"

"We've got to find Sid," Bobby continued. "You know, give him some cash to keep him quiet." But I was sure—and I was sure that Bobby was sure: Sid had already talked. And that realization placed added urgency on this trip to my house. We'd need to get Bobby some clean clothes, gather a few things fast, and get out of there before the police arrived.

It must have been around 12:30AM when we pulled into the driveway. We lived in an old green farmhouse containing three apartments. A family, the Underwoods, occupied the front. My family lived in the apartment in the back. As we got out of the car, we could see through the window that the Underwoods were awake, sitting around their kitchen table—with Sid.

"Sid! Come out here," Bobby called, motioning with his hand. Sid didn't move. Neither did the Underwoods. They all looked scared; paralyzed with fear. And it was now obvious. Sid had talked. It was an icy and awkward couple of moments. I'm sure they were terrified, wondering—as I was wondering—what Bobby might do next.

We headed to the back where my family lived. Mom and Dad were asleep on the foldout in the front room. We snuck past, quietly. In just seconds, Bobby washed up some more and put on clean clothes, then we gathered a couple of things and made our way back out to the lady's Cutlass. Another pass by the Underwoods' window, and there they were. They hadn't moved. We knew that we had to.

It might have been 20 miles, over a lot of winding roads, from my house to Scranton. Again, I don't remember saying much. Bobby talked a lot, but about what I have no clue. Something about Sid. Something about having a plan. Something about going away. My mind wandered through it all. It was settling in; I was probably never going back to school. Football, track—two things I actually liked at school, and did well at—they were done for me.

The idea of leaving, though, was sort of appealing. I didn't really have anything at home to hold me. I'd spent the better part of my teenage years trying to avoid being home—leaving early each morning, staying late after school, hitchhiking to see girlfriends—pretty much staying away all hours of the day. A fresh start somewhere else sounded like a win, not a loss.

As we approached Scranton, the lady's car started to overheat. "Dammit!" Bobby said. "We need some water."

He pulled into a doughnut shop. You know the stereotype ... Who do you find afterhours at doughnut shops? We looked up to realize we'd parked next to a police cruiser, and two cops were sitting in a booth right inside the door. Bobby went in and asked the man at the counter for some water, throwing a thumb over his shoulder, "My car is overheated." The officers followed him out, offering to help.

They walked toward me—my cousin with two cops in tow—and Bobby remained cool. I felt like I was going to have a stroke! My face started to get hot; I was overheating just like the car! I was still a little drunk, but sobering up fast. I wondered if my face was turning red, if the cops could see panic written all over me.

"Thank you. We've got it," Bobby calmly told them. "Just needs a little water. Bad radiator. Happens all the time."

Bobby could talk a dog off a meat-wagon. He made small talk with them as he added water. The officers stuck around for a few more minutes, wished us well, then got in their car and left.

Bobby knew my heart was in my throat. "You've gotta calm down, Gene," he said. "I know just what you need."

We left the car there. It was a liability to us now. Bobby got on a phone and called for a cab. He asked the cab driver, "Where can we pick up a couple of girls?"

"Trotter's Motel," the driver replied. And with that, we were off.

We waited outside Trotter's while the cab driver went upstairs. He came back and told Bobby two girls were waiting. We went up, and the prostitutes told Bobby it would be $60 each. He paid them.

The next thing I knew, I was in a room with this girl taking her clothes off. It was a surreal experience—sort of like I wasn't really there, but was rather looking down on it all, watching it unfold. The girl stunk of cigarettes, masked with a lot of perfume. She was trying to make out with me. I couldn't get into it.

"Your friend paid for this," she said. All I wanted was to get out. When I finally broke free, Bobby demanded his money back. An argument ensued.

Some guy showed up—a skinny black guy with a Marines t-shirt on. Bobby said, "Who's this? Your pimp?"

He threatened the guy, "I'll kick your ass!" The pimp got wise. He left. After a few more minutes of arguing, Bobby gave up, thanked the girls, planted a kiss on one of them, and we left. We waited for another cab. It must have been about 2AM.

Before I knew it, we were headed to Wilkes-Barre. Bobby said he wanted to go find some girl he knew there. He checked us in to the Sterling Hotel. *Finally, I'd get some sleep. Would I wake up in the morning to realize this was all a bad dream? Would I get that fresh start?* Bobby got me my own room. My head hit the pillow. I was out.

Bobby was seven years older than me. He had been in trouble with the law before. In fact, it was just a few months earlier that he'd been released from a prison in New Jersey, where he served time for a failed robbery. As far as I knew, that was all there was to it.

He was a good-looking guy. He had blonde curly hair. He was short, but physically fit—big, muscular arms. He had an infectious personality. Always smiling, always laughing. He got along with everybody. Everybody liked Bobby.

Everyone except maybe my older brother Chuckie—he might have felt differently. One time, Bobby heard that Chuckie had struck his wife and shoved my sister Mary in a burst of anger. Bobby went right over to their house and punched my brother in the face.

I remember Chuckie calling us afterward, saying, "I'm over here with a steak on my face because of Bobby." I guess he learned a lesson.

And that was Bobby. He always came across as seeing things in black and white, straightforward. It still rings in my head, him saying, "You never hit a woman!"

My sister and I, we loved Bobby. He was the cousin who paid the most attention to us as younger kids, growing up. He was the fun-loving relative who, when he'd show up, would lift you with one arm, spin you around, make you laugh. He removed the caps off our soda bottles with his teeth—silly stuff like that. He made us feel special, like he was there just to see us.

That week, he'd come to visit us from his home in Jersey. He was there four or five days, staying at my brother Mike's place down by the lake. He came over to our house every night to hang out, play cards, and have a few drinks. He told us his wife and daughter would be coming to join him soon. Looking back, that part all seemed a little strange. But at the time, I was just thrilled Bobby was there.

My mom loved Bobby, too. He had always been very good to her, helping her out any way he could over the years. I remember one time—years before my mom met my stepdad—she was dating this guy where we lived in Beachwood, New Jersey. The guy turned out to be a real jerk. He was addicted to pornography, unfaithful to my mom. When she had finally had enough, she called Bobby to come and load all our belongings into the back of a U-Haul truck. He drove us to Pennsylvania, where one of my mom's girlfriends found a small two-bedroom apartment on a dairy farm for us to stay. It was always like that—Bobby was someone she could count on.

There's irony in that. I woke up in the Sterling Hotel—on the run from the law with my cousin Bobby—recalling that it was his assurance to my mom, "I'll look after him, Mary! Don't you worry. Nothing will happen! He'll be with me!" that had convinced her to let me go shoot pool at 11 o'clock with him at the Marine Room Tavern the night before.

When I opened my eyes in that hotel bed, the gravity of my situation rushed back in. Bobby had killed a woman, and we were on the run. Scenes flashed in my memory—the tavern, the victim, Sid and the Underwoods, me tossing Bobby's bloody clothes out the car window somewhere along the road. This was real. It had happened.

My thoughts were all over the place. *What had we done? And what were we going to do now?* It seemed to me there was no going back. All I could do was find someplace new and start over. Part of it, too, was that I didn't want to go home. Bobby was the guy I'd always looked up to, that I loved, that I believed in. He cared about me. I was going to stick with him.

I got up and found my way to Bobby's room. When he opened the door, I saw he had some girl in his bed. "We're going to New York City," he said. "She's coming with us." I think he said her name was Caroline, but I don't quite remember.

He invited me in while he got dressed. Bobby explained he had a friend in the city whom he'd met in prison. "This guy will know what to do. He can help us." Bobby sounded confident. So I was feeling pretty confident.

"Reports are out," he said. "We made the news. Your mom has been on TV this morning. She's talking about how they know I killed the old lady, and they just want you to come home."

Home? I imagined that now, home was where this adventure would take Bobby and me. Where he was going, I was going ... that would be home. But the thought of my mom, distraught, on television, embarrassed—her son and her nephew wanted for murder—I felt sick to my stomach.

"I also talked to Chuckie," he said as he put on his shoes. Chuckie—the one Bobby had punched—lived in Wilkes-Barre at the time. "He said he'd help us get to New York; has a ride arranged for us."

"Good," I said.

"No, not good!" Bobby replied. "I checked it out. He's made a deal with the police. They're on to us. They're waiting for us to show up there." Chuckie had a couple simple warrants out for him; he must have thought this was his opportunity to make them go away. I don't know how Bobby knew that, unless he'd gone to scope it all out while I was asleep—maybe on his way to pick up this girl, who was now up and had her back turned to us, putting on her clothes.

We'd leave the police waiting for us over at Chuckie's place. Bobby decided to catch a bus to New York instead. We gathered our few things—and Bobby's girl—and ducked out of the Sterling Hotel, headed for the Greyhound Bus terminal.

The next Greyhound bus to NYC didn't leave for several hours. Bobby worried the police might wise up after a while and come looking for us. We didn't have hours to wait. So we walked a few more blocks to the Trailways station, where a bus was just getting ready to pull out. We got on it, bound for

New York's Port Authority Terminal.

The bus ride took a couple of hours. I remember Bobby was occupied with his girl. I was still piecing together scenes from the night before. I wondered, too, about how the news was dawning back home. *My mom was on television?* That's about the last thing I could have imagined—cameras and reporters at my house. *What were my friends hearing? What were they thinking?*

When I could steer my thoughts to the future, I daydreamed a little about a fresh start. *Canada maybe?* I wasn't sure how the idea got planted in my head, but I imagined Canada might offer Americans on the lam a place for safe haven or refuge. New York City was a stopover, I imagined, until I could run to the border.

On a Friday afternoon, Port Authority was bustling with people of all different shapes, sizes, and colors. And they were all headed somewhere in a hurry, with schedules to keep. I'd never experienced the hectic pace of the big city before. Taking it all in was a welcome diversion for me, occupying my mind, momentarily, away from my own situation.

As we stepped out in the streets of New York City, the sights—and the smells—overwhelmed me. The scent of exhaust and food vendors, the unmistakable stench of urine from every alley we passed ... people everywhere, moving every direction ... it was a lot to take in. On one corner there were Hare Krishnas offering flowers and distributing pamphlets on nirvana. On another there were prostitutes, busting out of too-tiny tops and too-mini mini-skirts—leaving little to the imagination. Drug dealers were wheeling and dealing right out in the open, hollering at passers-by like they were legitimate street vendors.

I followed Bobby. Aside from stopping every-so-often to make a call from a payphone, he seemed to know where he was headed. We ducked into a fast-food joint for a bite to eat. Bobby was back on the phone. We stopped into a corner store and grabbed a couple pints of Night Train. Bobby was back on the phone. As the day wore on, it was dawning on me: he didn't know where he was going. We were wandering.

Bobby came upon a couple of skinny black guys on a corner and had a brief conversation. He bought some marijuana from them. Then he asked about heroin, and one of the guys said, "Yeah." They led the three of us down an alley and up into a nasty old building.

I was pretty buzzed by then from the Night Train, but sober enough to know we were walking into a bad scene. I worried—Bobby was carrying all our cash. *What if this was a set-up? What if these guys jumped us, robbed us?*

It was a raggedy old place. It looked like it ought to have been condemned. Might have been, now that I think of it. Inside it was dark and rancid—a mixture of mold, dampness, human body odor, urine, you name it. This place was what they call a shooting gallery, a one-stop shop where you can buy drugs, prepare them, and shoot them up with all the equipment provided.

There were half a dozen people lying around, a few more crashed in dark corners. There were take-out containers, filth and dishes, worn-out furniture, cockroaches crawling all over the place. I asked to use a bathroom only to find a man, passed out, sitting on the toilet. When I came back, they were cooking up some heroin on a spoon.

"Want some?" Bobby asked. I shook my head no.

This was way over my head. I drank a lot and even smoked some pot before, but sticking a needle in my arm—I couldn't imagine it.

Bobby persisted. "If you don't want the needle, you can snort a little bit." He dropped a little powder on a table and handed me a rolled-up dollar bill. "Go on!" he said.

I put the bill to my nose, leaned over the powder, and inhaled. I didn't feel anything out of the ordinary. I was actually relieved.

Things were going from bad to worse. Once the dealers had cooked up the heroin, they turned to find a couple sleeping on an old stained, threadbarren mattress.

"Hey! Get up!" they shouted. When the two were chased from their slumber, they flipped the mattress up against a wall, revealing holes cut in the back of it, housing their stash of needles and ligatures.

"Knot up!" one of them said. Bobby took what looked like a shoestring from their stash and tied it around his upper arm. He used one hand and his teeth to do it, like he'd done this many times before. I started to realize this life—the streets, the drugs, the hustles—it was really Bobby's world. I watched them put a dirty needle to the spoon, draw the heroin up into it, flick the side of the needle, and then hand it to my cousin. Bobby injected it.

Within seconds, he was sweating profusely.

"Are you okay?" I asked.

"Oh yeah ... great!" was his reply.
Caroline was next. Same routine.

I was in disbelief. All I knew was that we needed to be making progress on where we were going, what we were doing. *What were we doing* here? When we entered this building, I was worried these guys might try to take our money. Now I worried Bobby might blow it all on drugs before we left.

When we finally emerged back onto the streets, it was dark—nighttime in the city. I'm not sure if it was still the alcohol, having snorted that powder, or some combination of both, but I started feeling pretty mellow. Worries faded. All the lights and activity mesmerized me. We wandered some more.

"My friend can't help us," Bobby finally confided. "He's hooked up with some woman. Turns out it's his old probation officer." And then he added, "Don't worry."

I didn't know what they were, but Bobby assured me he had other plans for us—this wasn't bad news. "We'll get a room for tonight."

We walked into a motel in Spanish Harlem. An old Asian man sat at the front desk—in a cage. "Seven dollar for room," he said. We giggled. Bobby paid for two. This place didn't look much better than the shooting gallery.

I said *good night* to Bobby and his girl. When I got to my room, I found the door didn't seal all the way—I could see out into the hallway even when it was closed. I crawled onto the lumpy bed and watched roaches race across the room's surfaces and up the walls. The drugs and the booze had at least, for the moment, numbed my conscience.

It had been a whirlwind 48 hours. I could have never imagined on Thursday afternoon the turn my life would take later—the night it all started.

My friend Dwayne and I had been working that day—a little farm job to earn a few bucks. After work, we were out in his dad's El Dorado. We'd stopped in at the Marine Room because we knew it was possible for minors to buy beer there—we'd had good luck a couple of times before. I walked in and asked the lady—the very same lady Bobby would kill—for an eight-pack of pony bottles. She served them up, I paid, and Dwayne and I were off, parked up the road to share our score.

I recalled our conversation. Sports. Girls. School. Who'd have thought that in mere hours I'd be fleeing a murder rap? We sat up that dirt road, drinking and talking until dark. Then Dwayne took me home.

At the house, everyone was gathered around the table, drinking and playing pinochle—my mom and dad, sister (Mary), Bobby, and my stepbrother Sid.

Sid was one of my stepfather Loren's 13 kids. He was a couple years older than me. We got along well enough, but weren't really close. When my mom married Loren, a few of his kids—including Sid—tried to come live with us. It was just too many people in such a small apartment. It lasted maybe a couple of weeks. They moved back with their mom on the Coolbaugh family land, across the Susquehanna, not far away.

Sid quit school early—was uneducated and unkempt. He was a pretty good mechanic. His clothes were always sort of dirty; he had dirty hands and grease under his fingernails from working on cars. He had a car of his own, so he came and went as he pleased. And Sid drank a lot. In most of my recollections, he was either drunk or well on his way.

I wasn't much for playing cards or family gatherings. But I sat around with them for a bit. It must have been around 10 o'clock when my parents said *good night* and went to bed. Bobby offered to teach me how to play poker.

We continued around the table an hour or so, when Bobby piped up, "I feel like shooting some pool."

I agreed, saying, "I want to go!"

Overhearing us, my mom, resting on the foldout in the main room, called out, "It's too late, Gene. You stay in, now."

I looked at Bobby as if to say, *Do something!*

And he did. He went to work persuading her to let me go. In a matter of minutes, we had piled into Sid's car and were on our way.

"Let's go to the Marine Room," Bobby said. It was a little strange, as there were some other places, closer, where we typically went to shoot pool. But I knew I would likely get served alcohol at the Marine Room, so that suggestion suited me.

There was one old guy sitting at the bar when we walked in. He was representative of the regulars there—middle-aged and older, vets, and all on a first-name basis around town. He was shooting the breeze with the lady behind the bar. We ordered some drinks and settled in around the pool table on the far side of the room.

Bobby and Sid were pretty good with a pool cue. I drank Peppermint Schnapps shots and a beer, watching them, for the most part. Bobby and Sid were drinking whisky. We were all really drunk. When the old man called it a night and left, Bobby handed me the cue and headed over to the bar.

He struck up a conversation with the lady—the owner, a woman named Belle. I was shooting pool with Sid, but conscious of the fact that Bobby and Belle were talking about puppies—there was a sign up that she had a litter for sale. "They're sleeping in the back room," she said. Bobby asked her to go get one. She did.

Belle came back a minute later and started fussing at Bobby, telling him to stay out from behind the bar. He told her he was looking for change, for the pool table or jukebox.

What had happened, I gather, was that when she left the bar, Bobby tried to open her cash register. She caught him. Their argument escalated a bit, and Bobby returned to the pool table with us.

"I'm going to rob this place," he said.

It didn't really sink in at first. Bobby persisted: "I tried to get the money, but she caught me. Come on! It'll be easy."

Sid and I told him we were out—we live here; that lady could identify us. "So we'll all leave," Bobby suggested. "I'll come back in alone."

I opened my eyes that Sunday morning and took a quick inventory. So far my life on the lam had amounted to a close call with police at a doughnut shop; a failed fling with cigarette-stained prostitutes; watching Bobby argue with a pimp; some girl named Caroline joining us; milling the streets of New York City; a drug deal in an alley; meeting an unconscious, half-naked man sitting on a shooting gallery toilet; snorting heroin through a rolled up dollar bill; witnessing Bobby and his girl shoot up; and experiencing all the comforts a cockroach-infested, seven-dollar-a-night hotel in Spanish Harlem can offer.

Reality dawned: Our money was running out, and, unless something changed soon, and drastically, my new start would be coming to an end.

It was probably about 9 o'clock when I went to Bobby's room. It was the same scene as the morning before in Wilkes-Barre—Bobby assuring me everything would be fine, while this girl, along for the ride, wrapped herself up in the sheets on his bed.

"I called your mom again," he said. "The cops tapped the phone, so I made it quick. I told her you are okay, that sort of thing. She wants you to come home."

"So what do you think I should do?" I asked, hoping Bobby would outline his game plan for us.

But Bobby didn't have one. He was content getting drunk, getting high, and cavorting around with Caroline. "Listen, Gene, it's up to you. You can stick with me, or you can go home—tell them it was all my idea, my fault."

That wasn't what I wanted to hear. I didn't know what to do. I was lost.

It was a sad awakening—my perspective of Bobby was changing. He'd been my hero, my rock. For the first time since this ordeal began, I felt like I was on my own. I'd need to make a decision now about my future, and I'd have to face the consequences alone. I didn't want to—I had no choice—but I was going home.

Around noon, we were back at the bus terminal. Bobby bought me a ticket on the next bus back to Scranton. He made another quick phone call to my mom. He told her he was putting me on a bus and when to expect me. I was really emotional, on the verge of tears. It felt like I was watching a movie about somebody else; I couldn't imagine this was *my* life.

As soon as he hung up the phone, he turned my way. This was good-bye.

He said, "Gene, I gotta go. They know where we are. They'll be here any minute. You tell them it was all me. Do you hear me? Do whatever it takes to clear yourself."

He gave me a quick hug, slapped me on the back, and took off into a dead run down the bus terminal, his girl in tow.

I stood leaning against the wall of windows lining the terminal. I was exhausted and dirty from our two days of running. My head was spinning. I really had no clue what awaited me back in Pennsylvania. Home didn't seem so bad after two days like this. I was sort of looking forward to the ride home, imagining my mom there to pick me up when I arrived—then a shower, a change of clothes, a bed.

It couldn't have been more than a minute or so—police officers, guns drawn, surrounded me. One of them had a picture of me in his hand.

"Are you Eugene McGuire?" he shouted. At the same moment, a stranger, who happened to be just a few feet away, was wrestled up against a wall. "Are you Robert Lobman?"

Poor guy was just in the wrong place at the wrong time.

"That's not my cousin Bobby," I said. "He already left." The stranger's eyes met mine for an instant. I can only imagine what was going through his mind!

"Where did Lobman go? When did he leave? Which way? What is

he wearing? Who is he with? Is he armed?" Their questions came fast and furious—and then they broke off running in the direction I told them Bobby had gone.

One officer stayed behind. "Are you Eugene McGuire? Are you intending to go back to Pennsylvania and surrender yourself to the authorities there?" I assured him I was. He stayed with me until I got on the bus.

CHAPTER 2

TELL THEM THE TRUTH, EUGENE

Just getting out of New York City was an adventure. Even though it was a Sunday, streets were busy and congested. I marveled that the driver could maneuver that big bus through the maze of obstacles without hitting any of the taxicabs, bicyclists, and pedestrians weaving in and out. I looked forward to the traffic clearing; getting on the highway. I was relieved to be headed home.

Once we got out of the city, things got pretty quiet. Too quiet, really. My thoughts returned again to the events of that night. Graphic recollections. Bobby shouting. Stomping. Blood.

I started asking myself different questions. *What if I had stayed home? What if, like my mother wished, I'd just agreed that it was too late and gone to bed?*

What if I'd have tried to talk Bobby out of it? What if we'd have just gotten into Sid's car and gone home, instead of allowing Bobby to go back to the tavern?

What if I'd have gone back in with him? Could I have stopped him?

The plan was to say 'This is a robbery!' and take the money. It wasn't to kill her. *How did this happen?*

I also briefly wondered how things might have gone had Sid kept his mouth shut. *Would we be in the clear now? Would we have gotten away with it? A woman was dead—would my conscience have let me live with that? Could I have gone on as if nothing happened?*

Then my thoughts turned even darker. *What would Bobby have done if Sid had come outside that night? We knew he called the police. Did he really want to give Sid a share of the money? Or was that just to draw him out?*

What if the Underwoods had come outside? It was obvious Sid told them about the crime. Would Bobby have gone off on them all? I desperately wanted to think about something else—I didn't like where my imagination was taking me.

I was really naïve about Bobby at that point. I still thought this was all about what happened at the Marine Room. I didn't know, yet, that it was a wave of violent crime that had Bobby on the run. When he showed up at our house that week, none of us knew he was wanted in New Jersey for murder, robbery, and grand theft—he'd apparently even bitten some guy's thumb off. The next 24 hours would bring a lot to light.

We were a little more than an hour into our trip when the bus pulled into the East Stroudsburg station. A handful of people got off the bus. Two men who looked to be in their 30s came aboard and began talking to the driver. I looked away for just a moment. When I turned back, one of the men had slid into the seat next to me. He was wearing jeans, a pressed shirt, and shiny shoes. "Are you Eugene McGuire?" he asked.

He introduced himself to me as Corporal Michael Jordan of the State Police Barracks in Tunkhannock. He said he would be riding with me the rest of the way.

"Your mother is waiting for you at the bus station in Scranton," he said. "You'll be able to see her as soon as we arrive." I can't recall if I said anything in reply. I stared out the window. I knew he wasn't riding along with me as Pennsylvania's ambassador to ensure my comfort. This was going to be more serious than Mom picking me up at the bus station and taking me home in time for supper. And I suppose I was ready. Ready to answer for the events of that night at the Marine Room Tavern, to get this burden off my chest.

As we approached Scranton, I began to feel really uneasy. It dawned on me that I was back—Bobby was on the run, probably strung out in some drug den in New York City, while I would be forced to answer for his actions.

Corporal Jordan said, "When we pull into the station, just stay put. We're going to let everyone off. Then your mom will be brought on the bus to see you."

We parked, and I watched as the bus slowly emptied. Once everyone was off, another officer got on, and then my mom stepped onto the bus behind him. She looked terribly distraught—absolutely worn out. Her face seemed to have aged several years with worry in just the three days since I'd seen her last.

Mom's eyes were puffy and red like she hadn't slept in days, or had been crying—likely both. Tears filled my eyes at the sight of her. When she got close, I could sense the pain and fear. She sat down next to me and gave me a hug. We cried. I felt her whole body trembling. When she finally spoke, she just said, "Tell them the truth, Eugene. You just tell them the truth." She repeated it over and over.

Corporal Jordan said, "Let's go," and as we stepped off the bus, an officer put handcuffs on me. It was both a surreal and sobering moment—I was in custody. I think I recall one of the officers even saying those very words on a radio: "We have Eugene McGuire in custody."

It was embarrassing, too. My heart ached for Mom, having to watch her son in handcuffs. I felt ashamed.

The officers sat me in the backseat of their car, and one of them read me my rights. It was like a scene on television, with their "You have the right to remain silent..."

But this wasn't a movie. It was real life. My life. At 17.

My formative years left much to be desired. My childhood, adolescence, and early teenage years were characterized by family dysfunction and drama. I don't share that as an excuse or to illicit pity, but rather to provide some backstory for context.

My biological father was a heavy drinker; you'd rarely see him without a can of Schaefer beer or a glass of port wine in his hand. It was a staple of his identity. Some of my most vivid recollections of that man were of him slurring and staggering.

He was a Catholic. What I recall of his Catholic faith was our going to church on Sunday mornings, and then straight to the bar after—my parents drinking until dark while my brother, sister, and I were told to entertain ourselves, playing pinball or music on the jukebox.

Mom divorced him when I was really young. He was rarely a part of my life after that ... and that was a good thing.

Then there was the guy my mom was seeing for a while in New Jersey. I can't recall his name. Which is okay. It's not worth mentioning anyhow. He was around just long enough to leave a mark on my young psyche.

In addition to his being a womanizer hooked on porn, he was also a racist. One vivid memory—I was probably about 10—was the time he walked outside and saw me shooting hoops. I was wearing a t-shirt on which I had written the name and number of my favorite Knicks player, Willis Reed, on the back.

"Why have you got a nigger's name on your shirt, boy?" he shouted. I had no idea what that meant, but the contempt in his voice, and the look of disgust on his face, crushed me. I took the shirt off and never wore it again.

I told you the story of Bobby helping us leave that clown and move to

Pennsylvania. What I *haven't* told you was what happened as we left.

I'd never seen my mom so hurt and angry. The guy had an old dirt track car he loved to tinker with in the garage. When we were packed and ready to leave, Mom walked out to that car and dumped a five-pound bag of sugar in and all over the top of that car's carburetor and intake manifold. (Good luck getting that engine to run again!)

Mom then married my stepfather, Loren, when I was 12. Loren was a Christian and a real gentleman. It may have been a love-at-first-sight sort of thing—they married pretty soon after they'd met. You could tell he loved my mom. We witnessed it every day in his words and even more in his actions.

Even when Mom and Loren would disagree, he'd treat her with gentleness and respect. I remember he'd say, "Trust the Lord, Mary. Trust the Lord."

She'd get so frustrated that he wouldn't bite at the chance to fight. She'd reply, "I can't even argue with you!" He'd smile. No doubt, he was a good man to my mother.

Loren was nice to us kids, too. He always told us old country stories and busted out unexpected rhymes. He made us laugh. We could tell he really cared about us, in spite of having 13 kids of his own. We agreed to call him Dad.

Though he was fun and loving, Loren never really spoke purposefully into my life, or into specific struggles or issues I had growing up. It may have been the awkwardness of being a stepparent and not my real dad. But I would have benefitted, I think, had he been more assertive with me.

Loren exemplified hard work. He worked long and difficult hours on the farm—he'd be up before the sun in the morning and have milked 30 cows before breakfast. His work paid for the farmhouse apartment roof over our heads, and put the staples—meat and potatoes—on our table. We didn't have much else, but we never went to bed hungry.

Something else I remember about Loren: his morning routine. On occasions when I was up real early, I'd see him sitting on the side of his bed—the foldout he and Mom shared in the living room—reading his Bible by lamplight before he went out to work. That made quite an impression on me. Here was a man who gave more than lip service to what he believed.

I picked his Bible up a couple of times and thumbed through its worn pages. I was curious what drew him to read it, regularly, as he did. I couldn't make any sense out of what I read, but the picture of Loren, the attention he paid to that book, and the way it affected him, remain with me.

But alcohol, unfortunately, cast a very dark shadow over our lives growing up. Both my biological dad—who would eventually die of cirrhosis of the liver—and my mom were alcoholics.

Mom's drinking would begin when she rose in the morning and continue until she passed out at night. Mom was on state assistance. Much of that money must have gone to her beer supply. She could go through a case of Black Label beer in a day. We all knew it—her eyes would glaze, her speech would slur, she'd get wobbly on her feet. It continued even after she married Loren. He'd go to work, she'd go to drinking. That was life as we knew it.

I had always been closest to my mom growing up. But that started to change when I became a teenager. She stopped asking me about my day at school and whether I had any homework. I struggled academically. When I no longer had any accountability at home, those difficulties multiplied. Eventually Mom even quit asking me about my daily whereabouts. I could—and did—come and go as I pleased. In no time at all, I was completely detached from relationships at home. Family was a huge void in my life.

At school, track and field and tackle football offered me a place to belong, and a place where I could succeed. I was good at sports. I fit in. Athletics helped my academics, too. Sports served as motivation to work harder in the classroom—in order to stay on the field. I loved putting on my uniform and representing our school.

I developed a daily routine of my own. I'd leave early for school each day and then stay late after school for practices, avoiding life at home as much as I could. I hated it when practice ended. That meant it was time to go home. It was a lonely feeling to walk in the door each night. I'd try to avoid everyone, head straight to my room, lie in bed, and daydream about a better tomorrow.

Reminders of family dysfunction were never far away. One painful experience was when my biological father came to one of my football games. I had invited him. I wanted him to see me play, to be proud of me. He showed up drunk. He stumbled out onto the sideline and was staggering around.

The coach asked, "Whose dad is that?"

I had to try and get him corralled off the sideline and back to the seats. Everybody watched us. I was so embarrassed. I don't even remember the game itself.

I hated my life at home. I became resentful of the little apartment we lived in and the lack of material things we possessed. Friends of mine at school all had bicycles or even motorcycles to get around. I walked and hitchhiked. They gathered around their dinner tables and had meals together—they passed the butter! You cannot imagine how badly I wanted a normal, mundane experience like that, just passing food around the table. They talked. "How was your day?" "What did you do?" My life was nothing like that.

I began drinking around 15. Everyone else in my family did. Why not? Getting drunk numbed me to my reality, to my disappointments. After a few cans of beer, I didn't care anymore. Although I never wanted to smoke cigarettes, I tried marijuana with my brother, Mike, who was already pretty deep into drug use. He taught me how to smoke it—to inhale it and then to hold my breath. The weed made me relax, buzzed, and carefree. It was a huge improvement, I thought, over sorrow and self-pity.

One night I stayed out drinking until 2 o'clock in the morning. When I got home, my mother was waiting up. It was out of the ordinary—Mom would normally have passed out hours ago, oblivious to what time I came in. This time she was up, and she was angry. I must have gotten sarcastic with her. She swung to hit me. I blocked her first few attempts, which only made her angrier.

Finally, I grabbed both of her hands with mine and said, "You're not going to hit me!" She pulled her hands free and stormed out of my room. I went to sleep.

In the morning, Mom wouldn't even look at me. I knew I'd disappointed her. I knew I'd hurt her. I tried to apologize. When I did, she let me have it. Her yelling made it abundantly clear that she wasn't interested in my apology. I turned and walked out of the kitchen. I waited in my room for the school bus to arrive.

Owning my mistakes and apologizing for them has been hard for me ever since. *Who wants to hear it? Who cares? It won't make any difference.*

<hr />

"Tell the truth, Eugene. Just tell them the truth," Mom continued to remind me as we entered the State Police Barracks at Tunkhannock. It was a small, unremarkable one-story building—pretty sterile-looking, everything was gray.

They led us to the back of the building. There were desks in the room covered with manila folders, dog-eared papers, and police manuals. The place was a mess. They instructed my mom and me to sit down. We sat on one side of a table and watched as the detectives gathered pads of paper, pencils, and chairs to join us. My heart was pounding. I felt like I was going to explode. I just wanted to get this over with.

The detectives finally stepped over to the table, took their jackets off, and hung them on the back of their chairs. One of them leaned over and took off my handcuffs. I rubbed my wrists, thankful to be done with those restraints.

They settled in and nodded to one another—it was time to begin.

One of them spoke up: "Eugene, do you want to tell us about what occurred at the Marine Room Tavern on June 17th?"

Mom sat beside me. That was unsettling. She kept encouraging me to tell the truth, but there was a lot of the story I'd have preferred for her not to hear. Bobby had talked to her a couple of times on the phone. *What had he told her? How much of what I'd share would be news to her—news of her son and her favorite nephew that would crush her?*

I didn't know where to start. I waded into the story starting with the decision Thursday night, around my kitchen table, to go shoot pool. "It was me and Bobby and Sid," I began.

It had struck me as strange, you recall, the decision to go to the Marine Room. Sid told the police that decision was made because the woman there, Belle, cashed paychecks for her customers—there would likely be more cash on hand.

"Were you aware of that?" the detective asked me. No. I wasn't. It was dawning on me that this robbery wasn't some spur-of-the-moment idea Bobby had, but rather an existing plan he had drawn me into.

My thoughts and emotions were twisting and turning. I didn't want to sell out my cousin, but there were obviously parts of this story of which that I was not aware—parts that appeared more premeditated than coincidental. At certain points of my telling the story, the officers seemed to know more than I did. That was unnerving.

I walked the officers through the half-hour or so we were there, drinking and shooting pool, before the crime occurred. I told them of Bobby's attempts to mess with the cash register, and the woman catching him. I told them how Bobby came back over to us, determined to rob the place, and how reluctant Sid and I were of his plan. "I wasn't going to do it," I said.

"We left the Tavern, all three of us. We drove a hundred or so yards up the road, pulled over, and turned off the lights. Bobby was amped up and excited. 'Let's go!' he shouted. 'Let's do this!' When neither Sid nor I agreed, Bobby said, 'Fine! I'll do it myself!' and he got out of the car."

The recollection of that moment was so vivid for me—I could hear his voice. I felt both the adrenaline rush and the fear I experienced in that very moment all over again.

I didn't tell the cops this, but I was pretty excited about the picture Bobby had painted. I liked the thought of having some money in my pocket. I suppose as I watched Bobby walk back down the road toward the bar, I expected he'd be back in no time at all, cash in hand, and we'd be racing away, laughing about how easy it was.

I knew it was wrong. But I never imagined *this*. Swiping some cash from the old lady at the bar—that was all it was supposed to be.

"Bobby was really drunk," I told them. "We all were. But Bobby, most of all. As we watched him heading down the road, it was obvious. He could barely walk. So I climbed out of the backseat of the car and followed after him—thinking he might just fall over.

"He made it to the door. 'I'll be out in a minute,' he said. 'I'll knock her out and grab the money. I'll be right back.' Bobby disappeared inside. I stood in the parking lot, waiting. After a minute or two, Sid joined me. We waited together, probably 10 yards from the door."

"Then what happened?" a detective asked. I must have paused long enough for him to read my discomfort. "Would it be easier if your mom waited outside for this part?"

I nodded. They took a break for a moment and escorted her out to another room, before we'd continue.

"Go ahead," the detective said. "It's just us now."

"We heard banging," I started. "Banging coming from inside the tavern. It was loud. Me and Sid looked at each other, like *What is that?* There was a lot of banging around and it went on for what seemed like a long time. I decided to go peek in the door, to see what was going on."

The officer wanted to confirm the setting, "Bobby's inside. You're in the parking lot, moving to peek in the door. Sid's with you."

"Yes," I replied. "When I opened the door, it was dark—darker than usual, like someone had turned out the lights. The commotion was going on over to the left, where the pizza counter met the bar. Bobby was yelling, 'Die, you motherf......! Die!' and he was jumping up and down, stomping the victim under his feet. I saw him take a beer bottle and beat it on the side of the bar—the banging we'd heard—to break it off. He cut her with the bottle."

"A bottle was his only weapon?" the detective wanted me to clarify. "He didn't have a knife or anything else?"

"Not that I saw. Just a bottle."

"So Bobby killed the woman?" the detective asked.

"Yeah," I said.

"Was she screaming? Was she calling for help?"

"I never heard her. All I heard was Bobby ... and the banging."

"What did you do?"

"I yelled, 'Stop!' Sid and I were freaking out, panicked really. We backed out the door."

I really wanted to have more to tell the detectives about this moment. Truth is, we backed out the door, and I don't remember either of us saying a thing. I racked my brain trying to recall. That moment or two—from when we backed out and before I entered a second time—was gone to me. I had, and have, no recollection of it. From being scared? In disbelief? I have no idea.

"We stepped back in, a moment or two later," I offered. "I think the woman was dead. He was done with her. Bobby shouted at us to help him find the money. I did what he said. I looked around for money."

"Where's Sid at this point?" they wanted to know.

I had no idea. I hadn't thought about Sid once I stepped inside. I'd assumed he was doing the same thing I was, but I just didn't know. I realized then that from the moment I stepped inside I didn't see him again until he was sitting at the Underwoods' kitchen table.

As clearly as I could recall, I walked the detectives through the next 20 or so minutes of searching the tavern—what I remembered Bobby doing and what I remembered doing myself.

"Did Bobby rape the woman?" one detective asked. His question startled me.

"What? No way!" I replied.

The detective explained they'd found the victim with her clothing disheveled. I told them Bobby had searched her for a money belt and gone through her pockets, but that was all. I explained that we had searched everywhere—the cash drawer, behind the bar, the kitchen, and even in the storage sheds out back—before we finally found the cash box. I told the detectives that was the only time I'd seen the woman's body—when I looked over the counter, and when Bobby found the money stash.

"Sid left while Bobby and me were still inside," I told them. "That's when we saw her car and found her keys." I walked them through our trip back to the house, how we'd seen Sid with the neighbors.

They confirmed, Sid had indeed notified police. I also learned that the police were literally only minutes behind us. They arrived at the house just moments after we pulled out. They had tracked us to Scranton and into Wilkes-Barre, but when we changed bus terminals at the last minute, they didn't know we went to New York.

"We'll have Lobman soon!" one of them assured me. I didn't believe it. I figured Bobby would elude them forever. One of the officers went to bring my mom back in.

They asked about Bobby's clothing and the weapon. I knew nothing of the bottle—I supposed it was tossed away in the tavern. And his clothing: I had tossed it out the window of our car somewhere between home and Scranton.

All that was left to cover, at that point, was our trip to New York, through both Scranton and Wilkes-Barre. They asked about the girl Bobby took with us. I knew nothing about her, except I thought maybe her name was Caroline.

It was the strangest sensation recounting all of this for the detectives— at times it felt as if I was a witness, like I'd seen it, but not participated. At other points, and especially as the detectives asked pointed questions of my involvement, it was clear—I was a participant in this crime. A woman was dead. I shared in the responsibility, and the guilt, for her death.

After I'd finished telling the story, the cops took me back to the beginning again—this time asking me all sorts of questions, almost cross-examining me as to the facts. What I knew and what I didn't. They also told us a lot about Bobby we didn't know.

We had no idea he was on the run from charges in New Jersey when he showed up at our house that week. They painted the picture that he'd planned this robbery at the Marine Room simply to help him get farther, faster, as his crimes were catching up with him. I hated to imagine that was true—that Bobby had hidden anything from me, or, worse, used me. My mind was spinning.

The questioning went on for eight long hours. It was getting late. I was weary. Mom looked terrible. She'd been through the emotional wringer. Her expression was a mixture of confusion, uncertainty, and fear. I think she'd imagined when we entered this room, I'd tell the truth, and then we'd be able to leave; she'd take me home. I suppose I felt that way too. It was dawning on us both—I wouldn't be leaving with her.

When the interview was finished, one of the detectives told me to stand up. "Eugene McGuire, you're under arrest for the murder of Isabelle Nagy," he declared as he returned the handcuffs to my wrists. My mother began to cry. I was numb. Again, like a scene from a movie. I couldn't imagine this was happening to me. They let Mom hug me before they took me out of the room through a side door.

They led me down a hallway to be fingerprinted and photographed. My fingers and palms were rolled with black ink and pressed onto a heavy card-stock paper. They had me get two pictures—one straight ahead, the other a profile.

As all of it was taking place, I overheard detectives discussing where to take me. I listened as one called the juvenile detention facility to prepare a bed for me. My mind was racing. *What would happen to me there?*

CHAPTER 3

THE FIRST NIGHT OF THE REST OF MY LIFE

It's strange the things you do and don't remember decades after they've happened. Hours on a bus back from New York, eight or more hours of questioning by detectives—they must have fed me at some point. I don't recall. But I do remember the 40-or-so minute ride from Tunkhannock Barracks to the Luzerne County Juvenile Detention Center, locked in the backseat of the car. I was tired, but my mind was racing again.

One moment my thoughts returned to the crime—the hours-long interrogation with detectives and what I'd told them. The next my imagination kicked into high gear. Bobby had told me jail stories. *Would the detention center be like that? Who would I have to fight?* This was, after all, going to be a juvenile facility. Probably not so tough, I tried to reassure myself.

Then I'd flash back to New York City—roaches, drugs, traffic. *Had that really been me? Was I really there … just last night?* Twenty-four hours ago I imagined a new start in Canada. Now I was headed to Luzerne County lock-up.

I might have given a quick thought to escaping. I noticed there were no handles to open these backseat doors from the inside, and a thick safety partition separated the back from the driver's seat. The officers in the front carried on conversation, for the most part, as if I wasn't there. It was just a routine day at the office for them.

It wasn't routine for me. These roads we were winding down toward Wilkes-Barre, I'd traveled many times before. But I'd never imagined seeing them from this vantage point—handcuffed in the back of a detective's State

Police car, on my way to jail.

My mind flashed forward, too. *How would this end? Would Bobby be caught? Were the police really as close to catching him as they said? I couldn't believe it. They'd never catch Bobby. But if they did, would his capture and answering for the crime help my case? Would I catch a break? Would I have to testify against him? Could I?* I sort of imagined this might turn out to be just a close call for me, a real life lesson I could always look back on.

Then the cycle began again. Crime scene. Anxiety. Escape. *I can't believe I'm heading to jail! It will be okay.* Over and over.

As we approached the property, I could see Luzerne County jail at the bottom of a hill, the juvenile detention facility on the top. Around the front were offices and courtrooms. The car pulled through a fence and the officers prepared to walk me in.

The reality of confinement really sank in when they escorted me through a solid metal front door. It was opened for us, and closed behind, locked with a large brass key. They signed me over to an officer there, removed the cuffs and shackles from me, and left. It was a pretty terrifying moment. No familiar faces. *What would happen next?*

The man in charge looked over my paperwork. "Murder, eh?" he remarked as he looked up at me over the top of his eyeglasses. "You keep quiet about that in here, son. Do you understand me?"

I nodded.

"Just tell the others you're in here for shoplifting or stealing a bike or something. You got it?"

"Yes, sir."

Then he instructed me to follow another officer down the hall. I did, and he led me into a shower room. My heart was pounding—I could feel my pulse throughout my entire body.

"Do you have any contraband on you?" he asked. "Are you hiding anything?"

I assured him I didn't and I wasn't.

"Strip naked," he said, "and put all your clothes in this plastic bag." He handed me a bag and stared at me. "Let's go!"

The humiliation was only beginning. I stood naked before him. He looked me over thoroughly. I'd had a physical at the doctor's office before. Needless to say, this was quite a bit more intrusive. I'd never had anyone tell me to bend over and spread my cheeks before.

After the search he handed me a little plastic cup with yellow soap in it. He pointed to the showerhead on the wall. "Get to it," he directed.

The scent is one I'll never forget. This yellow goo had a strong chemical smell—sort of a mixture of lemon-scented disinfectant and bug spray. Come to think of it, that's probably just about what it was. They call it delousing. Its purpose is to kill anything that might be living on you. Once he was satisfied I was lice- and scabies-free, the officer handed me a towel and some jail clothing to put on. When I was dressed, he escorted me to a cell.

There was no light in the room. He explained that officers controlled when the lights were on and off—and it was late. "You'll get used to the routine," he promised.

I could make out a single bed and a folding chair. "Have a good night," he said as he locked the door and walked away. I sat down on the edge of the bed allowing my eyes to adjust to the darkness. As they did, I saw a porcelain toilet and sink over on the far wall. A tall window with bars was my portal to the outside world.

After a couple of minutes, I stepped over to the window and looked out. I could see the highway. I waited quite a while to see a car travel past. It was after midnight, now. There weren't many cars on the road at that hour. I felt abandoned and alone. Mom was back at home. I imagined she was wide awake with worry. Bobby was on the run—probably blowing the rest of the money. Here I was, behind bars, wondering what would happen next.

Then I noticed a neon sign across the road—it was a little tavern. I had to look away.

Morning brought what would become my routine for the next nine and a half months at the juvenile detention center. Not much changed from day to day. Morning meal, time in the dayroom, lunch, more time in the dayroom, supper, chores in the surrounding buildings (the offices and courtrooms I mentioned on the front side of the building)—we'd clean them and empty the trash at night—then lights out.

The juvenile facility was built to hold maybe 15 or so prisoners, but there were never more than four of five while I was there. The other kids came and went pretty quick—only a few days' stay and they would return to their families. I was an anomaly. I would remain there until my sentencing.

I was only there a few days when trouble interrupted my routine. An officer came and grabbed me out of the dayroom where I was talking to some of the guys.

He took me into the office where he told me, "You were supposed to keep your mouth shut! You told another kid why you were here, didn't you?"

I supposed I had. But the officer was quite agitated. I didn't understand why it was such a big secret. But I was rewarded with the next 10 days isolated in my cell to think about it—and by that time, a whole new crop of kids had come. From that day forward I resolved: while in juvie, I was a bike thief if anyone asked.

My attorney came to see me within those 10 days. He was a really tall, lanky guy. He had on a beige suit, a checkered tie, and fancy leather shoes. He carried a brief case, the kind with a little brass hasp lock on it. I didn't know what a lawyer was supposed to look like, but this guy looked too young to me, and sort of scared. He sat on the folding chair, while that big briefcase resting on his knees served as a sort of barrier between us. He began by saying this was his first murder trial—not exactly what you want to hear...

I had to walk through the story again, the first time for him. And with every re-telling, the scenes flashed vividly through my mind anew. The *What if?* and *If only...* arguments played out again, like an opera in my head.

Have you ever wanted to be able to go back in time to undo just one event? If only! But here I was, recounting the horrors to my too-young-looking and overmatched-by-the-case attorney.

He was a nice enough fellow, I suppose. He tried to sympathize with me—he said he understood what it was like to make bad decisions while drinking alcohol and to have a difficult life at home. He assured me that his first order of business was to persuade the court to understand, and to try me as a juvenile.

After my lawyer's first visit, my mom brought news. Bobby was back. He had surrendered to police. Apparently, his wife, Arlene, convinced him to come back to Pennsylvania and face the music. I imagined the money and the highs ran out—perhaps his sidekick prostitute left when the boozing and cruising came to an end. I wondered what this would mean to my case.

Just a day or so later, I was summoned to the Magistrate's office in Factoryville for a hearing. They put me back in street clothes, but by my hands were both cuffed and locked to a chain around my waist, and my feet were shackled. I was escorted in by two sheriffs, one of whom knew my family pretty well. He was kind and tried to prepare me for what I was about to experience.

"There will be cameras, Gene," he warned. "We'll walk you in. Just keep calm and try to ignore them."

He was right. When I stepped out of the car, the cameras surrounded us. People were asking all sorts of questions; I couldn't even make out what they were saying—we just walked.

There's a picture from the newspapers that day I've since seen. It takes me back. I hear the camera clicks, the voices, and recall the madness of it all. I also see how young I looked in that picture. My youth was about to come to an abrupt end.

When I arrived in the courtroom, Bobby and Sid were both there. I was surprised to see them. Bobby was surrounded by a slew of people. Sid had a single lawyer sitting next to him. I felt alone as the officers set me at a table by myself. After a minute or two, my lawyer joined me.

"This is just a formality, Gene," he said. "Sit tight."

The District Attorney, James Davis, read the charges against us. Murder. Robbery. Burglary. Theft. Conspiracy. He used many other ominous and incriminating words like *knowingly, willfully, feloniously, maliciously.*

What he actually read to the court is as follows:

As to the acts committed by the accused: Count 1, the defendants, Robert William Lobman, Eugene McGuire, and Sidney Charles Coolbaugh, did feloniously, willfully, and of malicious aforethought kill and murder the deceased, Isabelle Nagy; Count 2, that Robert William Lobman, Eugene McGuire, and Sidney Charles Coolbaugh did knowingly, willfully, and feloniously, in the course of committing a theft, inflict serious bodily injury upon another; Count 3: Robert William Lobman, Eugene McGuire, and Sidney Charles Coolbaugh did knowingly, willfully, and feloniously, enter a building or occupied structure with the intent to commit a crime therein, to wit, that they did enter the establishment known as the Marine Room with the intent of committing theft or a robbery therein; Count 4, Robert William Lobman and Eugene McGuire did knowingly, willfully, feloniously, and unlawfully take or exercise unlawful control over the movable property of another with intent to deprive her thereof, to wit, they did take, steal, and carry away a motor vehicle belonging to Isabelle Nagy and a quantity of money belonging to Isabelle Nagy."

Some of that—"kill and murder" for instance—sounded like it was included for dramatic effect. "Aforethought?" *Who says that?*

It sort of felt like another scene from a movie, but the gravity was real and palpable. This was me—my life—they were talking about. I had been involved in someone's death and was being held accountable. There were moments I wondered if it was real, or if it had all been a bad dream and that, at any moment, I'd wake up relieved.

Six or eight different detectives, including those who had questioned me, were on hand, I supposed, in case the judge had any questions for them. At certain points, the prosecutor turned and consulted with them privately over his notes. The three of us defendants and our lawyers remained silent. At the close of the hearing, the judge declared the offenses were not bail-able.

I was on my way back to detention. Never said a word.

My attorney came to see me a few more times before finally informing me the court had rejected his attempt to have me tried as a youth. I would be charged as an adult.

His demeanor turned pretty matter-of-fact at that point. "The best path you have of getting through this with even a chance to get out of jail would be to plead guilty to an open charge of murder," he said. "Agree to testify against Bobby and the charge won't rise any higher than second-degree ... perhaps it might drop to third-degree or even manslaughter. You could get out in eight to 10 years."

I was stunned. *Plead guilty to murder? Yes, I was there—but I didn't murder anyone. Couldn't I plead guilty to some lesser crime?* As I look back on it, all these years later, it seems likely to me that my lawyer just wanted to close this case and get it off his desk. The longer and friendlier dialogues, the understanding and empathy, were no more. Now it was ultimatums.

"You want a jury trial, Gene, you can do that. Plead innocent and take your chances. But I'm telling you, it will be first-degree murder without the possibility of parole. Do you hear me? That's the reality."

"Eight to 10 years?" I asked.

"That's what guys are getting," he agreed.

He'd say things to me like, "Let's make it easy on everyone." At the time, I had no idea what a trial was or what it would entail. He told me he'd seen a study that guys sentenced to life were getting out in eight to 10 years. *What's the point of saying "life" then?* He used words like *commutation*—no idea what that meant.

"This is the best path," he assured me, "for everyone's sake. Agree to testify against Bobby, do your eight to 10, and get out— get on with the rest of your life."

There I was, sitting in the dayroom in juvenile detention—a bike thief, if anyone asked. In reality, charged as an adult for murder, advised to plead guilty.

Three months after my arrest, I formally entered a guilty plea in court and agreed to testify against my cousin. It felt, at the time, like a betrayal. Bobby had told me before, when we parted ways in New York City, "Tell them it was all me, Gene." But the prospect of doing it soured my stomach.

What would it mean for me? What would it mean for him?

And Sid—he was a strange twist in all this. Sid had gone from witness to suspect in the crime. That first night I'd heard that Sid called the police and said, "They killed her!" When the police interviewed him at the Underwoods' home, they believed him to be the state's key material witness. Evidently, the more he talked, the more it dawned on them that he wasn't just a witness, but a co-conspirator and accomplice in the eyes of the law.

When I look back and couple my recollection with little things I've heard over the years since, it does seem that Sid and Bobby may have hatched a plan before we went to the Marine Room that night. The choice to go there instead of another spot wasn't a coincidence. Perhaps Sid had been the one who told Bobby the lady cashed checks—there would be a larger amount of cash on hand. But Sid wasn't in on the killing. Like me, he had no intention of harming that lady—no intention to be an accomplice to murder—and that's certainly why he high-tailed it out of there when we realized what Bobby had done.

Having pled guilty, I would have no trial. My attorney told me that I was pleading to an "open charge of murder," which meant the judge would assign its degree—assuring me it would not rise higher than second. A first-degree murder designation could carry the death penalty. It was off the table. The judge could assign third-degree or manslaughter, all the better. Whatever they'd decide to call it, I had my expectations fixed on eight to 10.

The court ordered an evaluative summary be done on me prior to sentencing. I have that document today—it seems like another life, another lifetime.

"The defendant was born to Mary and Eugene McGuire," the report begins. It introduces my whole family and the years up to my parents' divorce—my childhood in New Jersey. It reads, "While living in New Jersey, the defendant often visited and played with his older cousin Robert Lobman. The defendant states that he always admired and looked up to Bobby because he was older, and never afraid." True.

The report goes on to include mention of my high school records: "The coaching staff had high praises for the defendant's athletic prowess and had high expectations for possible outstanding achievements in this area." They must have been asking about my temperament, too ... "The staff stated that the defendant exhibited calmness and good judgment when under stress and pressure."

I suppose if I allow myself to think of it, I wonder what those interviews were like—my coaches, approached by someone from the court, asked, "What can you tell us about Gene?" It must have been like those things you see on television, where the next-door neighbor says, "He was always such a nice young man. We never would have imagined he could do this!"

And they did talk to my neighbors. They approached people who had employed me at odd jobs after school, on weekends, and during breaks. "He is described by one of his former employers as 'a real go-getter.'"

It felt good to know that people held a high opinion of me back then. *How had I taken such a wrong turn?*

The report mentioned my consumption of alcohol. Apparently I told them I didn't believe I had a problem with alcohol, that I just drank frequently. They tied my most recent drinking—the days leading up to the crime—into Bobby's visit, saying, "The defendant's admiration for his cousin bordered on idolization."

Bobby and the alcohol—that's what they wanted to attribute my involvement to. Apparently I told them that had I not been drinking, I never would have allowed harm to come to the victim. I like to believe that's true. And the report ended by saying, "The defendant presently feels great sorrow over the victim's death, and even a greater sorrow over the way in which she met her death."

It is not lost on me. Isabelle Nagy lost her life that night. I wish I could have stopped it. Sid testified that when we stepped in and saw Bobby beating her, I shouted, "STOP!" I know I was in disbelief. Bobby—the guy who instilled in me "You never hit a woman, Gene!"—was killing her. What in the world had happened?

It was to be yet another telling of the story, but this time I'd be guided by the well-crafted questions and leadings of prosecutors. They wanted to break the story down into bits, sound bites, for the benefit of the court.

Bobby had a good lawyer, but there wasn't really a defense to present. He'd pled guilty to murder and robbery. So this hearing in which I was called to testify was a "degree of guilt hearing" before a panel of three judges. The death penalty was on the table. This judicial panel could sentence Bobby to die.

Sid was called to the stand before me. Prosecutors walked him through his recollections of that night. The three of us, the ride to the Marine Room, drinking, a game of pool—it was all sounding like a night of innocent fun until they got to Bobby brutally murdering Isabelle Nagy.

I listened as Sid testified, but my mind wandered a bit, too. I noticed the clock on the wall. Here I was sitting in court, while just four blocks away my friends and classmates were wrapping up a school day, preparing to be dismissed. *How did I get here? How did this happen?*

Suddenly I was jarred back into reality. Chaos erupted in the courtroom. "I'll kill you, motherf...!" Bobby shouted. "You hear me? I'll hunt you down and kill you!" Bobby leapt to his feet and grabbed the microphone from the middle of the defense table and hurled it in Sid's direction. The microphone's cable mercifully stopped it just inches from Sid's face.

Bobby's lawyer ran for cover. A throng of deputies descended on Bobby to subdue him—jumping on his back, grasping his legs, attempting to wrestle him back down into a chair.

"Control yourself, Mr. Lobman!" the lead judge ordered. Bobby yelled back, "I'll kill you too, Judge!"

It took several minutes for order to be restored. Additional deputies came in—a detail of them escorted Sid out past Bobby, who was still muttering murderous threats under his breath. A few deputies remained stationed right behind him, and would stand there, at the ready, for the rest of the hearing. And it was all the prelude to my taking the stand.

I was nervous—my heart was pounding, hands were sweating, stomach was in knots. Not so much because of what had just happened, but: Bobby was my cousin, I loved him. He had sent word to me through my mom to tell the truth. It still felt like betrayal.

"Mr. McGuire, how do you know the defendant?" the questioning began.

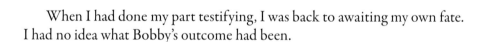

When I had done my part testifying, I was back to awaiting my own fate. I had no idea what Bobby's outcome had been.

March 8, 1978, was my day. It may have been on the way to my sentencing that sheriffs told me: they unanimously found Bobby guilty of first-degree murder. He had received life imprisonment for murder and 10 to 20 years for robbery—years to be served concurrently. In other words, he would never see freedom again. They said he was sent to Fairview, where convicts who were criminally insane were sent. I wondered if he was playing—or if he really was.

I also learned that Sidney had pled guilty and was awaiting his sentencing.

It was a Wednesday morning when they brought me in. My mom was there—I don't really remember who else. It was another shameful moment. I loathed the fact that my mom had to see her son, here, like this—hands cuffed, feet shackled—being sentenced for murder. The court spent a few minutes doing some legal housekeeping, all of which was lost on me. My lawyer was given a moment to speak.

"He's a young man, by doing the right thing he will be released at some point. It's a tragedy with the lady's death. It's a tragedy with this young man, too."

I'm not clear just what he was trying to communicate. It was obvious he wasn't making much of an impression on anyone.

Eventually the judge ordered my attorney and me to rise.

I don't remember anything the judge said beyond the words "second-degree murder" and the phrase "the rest of your natural life." It hit me like a hammer between the eyes. That's a far cry from eight to 10.

There was some commotion. More housekeeping as the judge, prosecutor, and my attorney spoke back and forth. My mom sat crying just a few feet from me. My lawyer was rambling on about my potential for being rehabilitated, the things included in my evaluation. *Was he saying it for my benefit? The courts? His own? Was he trying to appear as if he'd actually done something to help my case?* Too little, too late.

"The rest of your natural life..." What more is there to say?

Somewhere within the post-sentence exchange, the judge ordered I be remanded to the State Correctional Institution at Camp Hill to serve my sentence. I'd have to break it to my fellow juvies—the bike thief was leaving juvenile hall.

The two sheriffs who took me from the courthouse back to the juvenile detention facility immediately after my sentencing would return the next morning to transport me to Camp Hill. I had called Luzerne's 7x9-foot cell and the daily routine home for more than nine months. This was my last night there.

Immediately fear and anxiety rushed in with the realization: I was leaving in the morning for real prison.

Everything Bobby had told me—what he had written to me when he was in prison in New Jersey—went off like fireworks in my mind. Fist fights. Intimidation. Rape. Men who gave in—and even started dressing like women, wearing make-up—became "girlfriends" to other inmates. *Who would I need to fight? How soon after I arrived? Would I be assaulted? I wasn't going to become anyone's girlfriend!*

He had talked about drugs. Gangs. Race tensions. He had talked about guys watching each other's backs, getting in with the right crowd. *Would I get into the right crowd? How would I know how to recognize them?*

Bobby also talked about boxing and weight-lifting. Basketball. I tried to focus on those things. *I could get into that. Sports.* I even wondered about school—maybe I could study, get my diploma, make good use of the time. Those things were so much more pleasant to think about.

Nevertheless, my mind would run back: *I'm not the biggest guy. I'm young. I'm white. I'm doomed.*

The two-hour ride to Camp Hill was quiet. Neither the sheriffs nor I had anything to say. One of them broke the silence near the end of the trip, telling me when we reached the top of the hill I could look down and see much of the prison. I leaned forward, with fearful anticipation, and looked through the windshield from the back seat.

It was enormous. A compound surrounded by rows of chain-link and razor-wire fences. There were dozens of brick buildings in perfect rows. Tall smoke stacks that stood out and a recreational yard I could see in one corner.

It was all sitting in the middle of what looked to be farmland—it really looked out of place, like it didn't belong.

I remember making a conscious effort to calm myself down. *Breathe. I was going in there. There was no avoiding it.*

As they drove down the hill toward the prison, I watched out the side window. At eye-level, the long chain-link fence enveloped us. They pulled into the prison's parking lot and followed posted signs for "Prisoner drop-off."

I took note, now from the inside, of the tall fences and razor-wire. Nobody was going to escape this place. Red brick buildings, some measuring two and three stories tall, surrounded us. They reminded me of an old high school.

When we stopped, a small prison gatehouse stood in front of us.

I looked up and saw a prison guard patrolling, with a rifle, on a metal catwalk. He stopped and watched us closely as the sheriffs helped me out of the backseat. He scanned the parking lot as we approached the gatehouse entrance.

We stepped up to a thick metal door with a small window—the window itself was so thick it distorted everything on the other side. I saw what resembled an old man's face appear, heard a key turning in the lock creating a loud *clack*. A sound I'll never forget.

Indeed an old man greeted the sheriffs and directed them to bring me in and sit me down on a wood bench, gesturing in the general direction. The officers took a few minutes to sign papers, making small talk and laughing. I had a lump in my throat. The uncertainty of what was ahead played cruel tricks on my mind; my imagination went into overdrive trying to fill the void.

I attempted to steady my mind by looking around. I don't know what I expected the place to look like, but it reminded me of a bus station. Some wooden benches, vending machines—everything from cigarettes to sodas to snacks. A number of small windows, all held in metal frames. Although I could tell it was an older building, the place was pretty clean—in fact, it smelled like soap. The floor shined under a thick coat of wax.

Sheriff Truesdale, one of the two officers transporting me, had been a friend of my mother and step-father for years. He had me stand up, turn around, and kneel on the bench so he could remove my ankle shackles and handcuffs, as well as the chain from around my waist. Having been restricted for the last few hours, it felt great to have them off.

Then he turned me around. "Best of luck to you, Gene," he said. I could tell he cared. He produced a $20 bill from his pocket. "Use this to purchase a few things from the commissary to get you started." He looked me right in the eye and shook my hand.

When the door closed behind Truesdale and the other sheriff as they left, my fears heightened. I felt abandoned again, helpless. I was in a strange place far away from home. Nobody here knew me. There were thousands of prisoners here. *Would the world forget about me?*

That freedom from cuffs was short-lived. An officer in a very faded blue and gray uniform approached, ordering me to hold out my hands. He flipped handcuffs out of his belt and snapped them on.

"Sit down," he said, "until someone comes to get you."

I wondered who was coming. I didn't ask. He took a seat at a nearby desk and did some paperwork. I don't think he ever looked up at me again.

That metal door opened and closed a few times while I waited. Each time it did a cold wind rushed in. The thought crossed my mind: *I could run. I could blow right past the old man and be gone.* I sort of visualized it. But then ... *What was I going to do with these handcuffs on? Not to mention the guard on the catwalk and his rifle. The fences and the razor-*

wire. Nope. Folly.

So I sat. I waited.

It actually felt a lot like, and caused me to flash back to, that first night I spent in the juvenile jail back in June, nine months earlier. I felt helpless then. I felt alone. I had all sorts of worries and fears racing through my mind. Once again, *How in the world did I end up here?*

There is no way I can stay here. No way. I have to do whatever I can to get through this place, to get paroled. The truth had set in. *I wasn't going to be a high school senior. I wasn't going to graduate with all my friends back home. This is it—the rest of my natural life.*

Another loud *clack* echoed through the room. The metal door opened again. A corrections officer entered the gatehouse.

He handed the guy at the desk some paperwork and looked at me. "They keep getting younger, don't they?" he mused, shaking his head. Then he asked me, "Are you Eugene McGuire?"

I nodded and said yes.

"Follow me."

The route we walked was crowded with inmates coming and going from one place to another. An inmate shouted something about being queer to the officer escorting me.

Without missing a beat, the officer grabbed his crotch and shouted back, "I got your mother right here."

This was certainly not the dayroom at juvie.

We entered a building that was old, but the floors were shiny. The scent of lye soap filled the air. I was directed to sit on a bench where six other inmates sat awaiting their turn to be processed. *Was this my crowd?*

I turned to a man sitting next to me—he had a big, thick beard—and asked, "Where are you from?" I couldn't make out what he said. He mumbled. I asked a second time, he mumbled again. I smiled and nodded like I understood.

"Eugene McGuire," a voice called.

I stepped into a cramped Receiving and Discharge area. They gave me a card to fill out—an address to which they'd send my clothing. My heart began to pound again—I saw men just across the room, naked, showering. *Would this be another strip-search? I'd been searched coming and going from juvie, before transport—did we have to do this again?*

As intrusive as the juvenile strip search had been, this was worse. Besides the fact that complete strangers were looking at me naked, this time the search was ... how would I say it?... *Extremely thorough?*

"Open your mouth," he told me. He peered into my mouth, had me lift my lips, move my tongue. "Run your hands through your hair." I did. "Let me look in your ears." He glared as if he was looking deep into my skull. Then he studied my private parts meticulously. Then, you guessed it: "Now turn around, bend over, and spread your cheeks."

I wish I was kidding. And this was a routine I'd go through countless times—and it never ceased being humiliating.

Up next: a cup of delousing shampoo. "Hit the shower. Wash thoroughly."

After the shower, he had a wardrobe waiting for me. I put on the blue uniform and was told to grab the rest of my gear—three trousers, three shirts, three boxers, three t-shirts, three pairs of socks, one lightweight jacket, a towel, and a washcloth—and followed him.

Somebody with a big stamp—rubber bands with letters and numbers that turned—and an indelible ink-pad stamped my number, AK4192, on each and every item.

CHAPTER 4

HAPPY BIRTHDAY

Once the seven of us newcomers were checked in, deloused, dressed, fingerprinted, and photographed again, we were escorted to the Infirmary for medical screening.

Yet another stint of waiting—wondering and worrying about what was next. When my name was finally called to interview, I was surprised to see an attractive young woman would be gathering my information.

"What is your date of birth?" she began.

I hesitated for a moment. I couldn't believe it—"March 9, 1960," I said.

She wrote it down, then looked up at me, making eye contact. One of those pursed-lip smiles—like kindness mixed with sympathy—crossed her face.

"Happy birthday," she said without a hint of sarcasm. She was very genuine.

Do you remember your 18th birthday? What did you do? Who was the first person to say "Happy birthday" to you? Did you get cards? Did you get gifts?

I got strip-searched and in-processed at a state correctional institution. A girl I'd never met before—and would never see again—was the only person to wish me a *Happy birthday*. I got a card—with AK4192 printed on it—and a new prison wardrobe to match it.

After the medical screenings, we were escorted to C-Block, also called "quarantine" due to the fact that everyone arriving at Camp Hill spends 30 days there, apart from the general population. That was actually welcome news to me—I'd have a few days to let this place sink in before stepping into the real worrisome environment.

As the seven of us walked through a large concrete corridor, there were inmates walking up and down. Everyone slowed their pace to stare at us. We were the new fish. The guys in quarantine wore blue. Everyone else was in prison browns.

Guys were cat-calling out to us. I was afraid but trying not to show it. The great unknown—I had no idea what to expect. *Would I have a cellie—a roommate? Would I have to fight any of these guys? When? Today? Tomorrow?*

As we walked, an inmate next to me recognized a friend of his in population. He asked him for some cigarettes, and the officer walking us in permitted it. It seemed fitting—the scent of the place took hold—a pungent mixture of stale cigarette smoke and ... cleaning chemicals. It seemed to calm him a bit that he knew someone here—had a friend on the inside. Again, I worried. *I didn't know anyone here. Would people I know on the outside even remember that I am here? Would my friends forget about me?*

When we reached C-Block, we stood in the hallway waiting for an officer inside to slide open the large metal door containing a small, pie-hole sized security window in it. When the key turned, I heard the familiar loud metal *clack*, and the door slid open on rollers to the side.

Inside were other men in blue uniforms like ours, working. They all stopped their activity to look at us, wondering if they would recognize someone in our group. Walking in, my eyes darted around the place, from end to end and side to side, up and down. The smell caught me again—a strong floor-soap smell, as if they'd just mopped. But it wasn't pleasant. It takes a long time to get used to.

The range was long, with cells running top and bottom all the way down it—two stories, with a metal-grated catwalk along the second floor.

We were made to wait again—each of us with our little boxes of clothing stood against a wall. "You'll each be assigned a cell," an officer said, "and given a three-by-five door card with your name and institution number. Place them on the outside of your cell when you get there."

Strangest thing—I remember the song *Baker Street* by Gerry Rafferty playing on the radio. It must have been a new hit. It played all the time. To this day I hear that distinctive saxophone melody and I'm taken right back.

One by one they called us into a storage area where we were given a pillow and a bed-roll mattress. When I stepped up, the officer said, "Cell 21 on range 1, McGuire," as if I should know what that meant. Noticing the direction everyone else was going, I just started walking, found my way down the range, and went into my cell. I put my name tag on the door: "AK4192."

Not a moment later, an officer came and shut the door behind me.

I said to myself, "This is it." And I thought about Bobby. *What would he do in this situation? How would he handle it?*

I'd heard about this transition at juvie. People said, "Once you get to correctional, you'll get a job, you can work toward your education." I tried to concentrate on those things—to put my mind on something positive. I wanted to get started, to move on.

I placed the mattress on the bed frame before me, sat down, and waited until they called us to come eat.

Sloppy Joe and french fries—that was my first prison meal. It was pretty good, actually. You're served on big metal trays, with a big metal cup. They load you up. I wasn't going to starve in here.

While I was in quarantine, the talk was all about what awaited us in general population. I heard all sorts of stuff about testing—how guys would try to intimidate you to see what you were made of. I heard about rape. In fact, I cut my hair real short—I wanted to be sure everyone knew I was a guy!

I'd heard about boxing in prison from Bobby, but also in conversation here. They had guys from Camp Hill that boxed in the pre-Olympic trials—one guy had even fought heavyweight champion Michael Spinks. He got knocked out, but that was beside the point. Boxing. I was up for that.

One day a guy named Amos, who had been in and out of Camp Hill a few times, walked by as I was shadowboxing.

"Boy, you're really workin' out!" he remarked.

"I want to get in on some boxing," I replied.

You know, you're gonna have your prison fights first, before you ever get in the ring. Oh yeah, we got a good development program here."

He laughed a sinister laugh as he walked away.

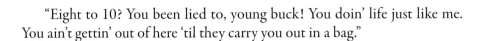

"Eight to 10? You been lied to, young buck! You doin' life just like me. You ain't gettin' out of here 'til they carry you out in a bag."

Intimidating words. The accompanying laughter made it even worse.

"Hey," he shouted to another inmate, "somebody told this boy he gettin' out in eight to 10!" More laughter.

I hadn't been there a month when I called my attorney. "I'm nervous because of what I'm hearing. These guys are saying I'll never get out of here. I want to go back to court." I explained to him that guys were laughing at me and telling me I got a raw deal. "The judge said 'the rest of your natural life!' He didn't say eight to 10!"

He got defensive. "I thought you understood that. You want to go back to court? You'll do more time, Gene. They'll make it first-degree murder like Bobby. They'll prosecute you for all the other crimes. By the time you're done, you'll never see daylight again. With the commutation process, you might get out in eight or 10 or 12 years."

Yeah, and I might not.

I hung up the phone defeated. That was the last conversation I'd have with my public defender.

Home. I'd spent my teenage years despising it. I'd done everything I could to be away—to stay away. I'd spent hours after school, at odd jobs, with friends. I'd even taken to hitchhiking to get to a girl's house, anything to not go home. It sank in: I wished, now, more than anything, I could just go home. There was really no place I'd rather be. For all of its faults and failures, that was home ... family ... my life.

This? This was unbelievable.

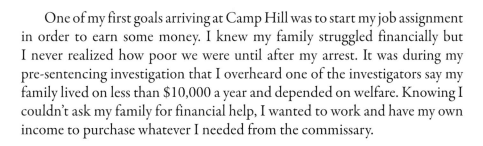

One of my first goals arriving at Camp Hill was to start my job assignment in order to earn some money. I knew my family struggled financially but I never realized how poor we were until after my arrest. It was during my pre-sentencing investigation that I overheard one of the investigators say my family lived on less than $10,000 a year and depended on welfare. Knowing I couldn't ask my family for financial help, I wanted to work and have my own income to purchase whatever I needed from the commissary.

A second goal was to earn my GED. I was really discouraged that I wouldn't earn a high school diploma and experience a graduation ceremony alongside all my friends. But prison staff told me a GED was its equivalent and was necessary for most of the better prison employment opportunities. They'd even have a graduation celebration for inmates completing the GED—family members would be invited to attend.

Before I knew it, my 30 days in quarantine was up. It was time to upgrade my wardrobe—I'd exchange the blues for prison browns, and every article of clothing stamped "AK4192" for when it went through the laundry.

It was also time to upgrade my accommodations.

"Gene, you're going to E-Block," I was told. "You'll be working in welding."

My first experiences of population, the range and the yard, were pretty staggering. There were probably 200 guys on the range. The Correctional Officers (COs) would open the door to the yard—guys could come and go as they pleased, the COs carefully noting who went out and who remained.

Fairly quickly I recognized things my cousin had told me about. It was actually just a couple of days before the crime that we'd sat talking about it— the guys who dressed like women, who Bobby said "wore punk panties." I couldn't imagine it then. Now—well, here they were. There were guys with kerchiefs in their long hair. They wore very effeminate clothing. There were even some guys wearing make-up and a few with shaved legs. One dude walked around wearing a t-shirt with an arrow drawn, pointing to his belly, over which he'd written the word "Baby."

It was so foreign to me. Out on the yard, there was a basketball court, guys playing ball over here; guys running on a track over there; an area of weights with guys lifting and working out over here; and then there was an area where all the guys who looked like chicks hung out, advertising their availability, I guess.

And you'd see it go down, too. They COs would unlock the cells, open the door to the yard, and, as guys were moving around, one of the cross-dressing guys would slide into another guy's cell and hang a privacy screen. It doesn't take much imagination to fill in the rest.

Walking into the main dining area for the first time was overwhelming. The only other cafeteria I'd ever been in was the school's—and it was nothing like this. There were hundreds of people sitting down to eat, and as many more still waiting in line for their food. It was loud—boisterous conversation, the sound of metal plates, cups, and utensils rattling—so loud, in fact, you'd have you raise your voice in order to even converse with the guy right next to you. It would take some getting used to.

The motion, too, was astounding. The serving lines in the chow hall were long but moved quickly. Everyone grabbed a tray off a cart and utensils out of a container as they moved through the line. As the food-serving containers on the line ran out, guys called linebackers quickly moved in to retrieve the empty eight-inch-deep metal trays and replace them with full ones. Fast moving. There was never any delay in serving the population.

As disconcerting as the noise and motion were, the smell of the chow line was halting. You know that wonderful smell of fresh baked bread or steaks cooking on a grill? Well, this wasn't close. It smelled like food—but it was more of grease and canned goods, mixed, of course, with that ever-present institutional cleaner scent. Crisco, pork-n-beans, and Pine-sol?

Inmates did all the cooking and serving for the 1,200 men doing time. Kitchen managers stood watch, as both supervisors and security. The rule was that whatever you accepted on your tray you had to eat. They never wanted to see guys waste food. An officer stood by the slop counters, taking note and confronting those who tried to throw away uneaten portions.

Food service is a job hundreds of inmates are assigned upon entering the prison system. It's easily the largest area of prison employment, serving the prison population and staff three meals a day. Working the kitchen detail is not a job anybody wants. It means long hours in a hot kitchen or standing over hot steam tables. Most guys who land that job go immediately to hoping for a transfer to another area—any other area.

I had a buddy named Scott who told me the story of his arrival at Camp Hill. A trouble-maker when he arrived, he was sent to the Hole for 60 days to cool his jets. Then they told him they had a cell for him in population, and a job in the kitchen. He turned it down saying he'd never work in the kitchen.

They gave him 30 more days in the Hole to think it over. At the end of that month they went again—a cell in population and a kitchen job. He refused again. The Hearing Examiner was furious and said, "Take this tough guy back to the Hole, this time for another 60 days!"

As he told the story, I was in disbelief. "You did two more months in the Hole over a kitchen job?"

Scott smiled and said, "No. I asked, 'Where do I pick up my kitchen whites?'"

Working in food service does have its perks. Those guys did whatever they could to hustle food, stealing steaks, chicken, and sugar. It could be pretty profitable for them. They'd bag up whatever they could get their hands on, sneak it back to the housing unit, and trade it or sell it for cigarettes. Some even used smuggled food items to make up meals using their own recipes. It was prison culture—what guys could do and get away with.

Speaking of prison culture, one of my first conflicts in the system started in the dining hall. It was during my first week in population, while standing in the long serving line, I noticed a guy staring at me from a table where he was sitting. He puckered his lips and blew a kiss at me. I looked away, hoping first of all that it wasn't intended for me, and, second, if it was, that he'd think I hadn't noticed. My heart pounded fast with intimidation.

Sure enough, a moment later I caught sight of him again. He repeated the gesture. *Hundreds of guys in this place, and I have to catch eyes with this guy blowing kisses.* I sized him up. Big black guy. Military haircut—high and tight. He was pretty good-looking, a muscular man—but I certainly wasn't interested. I was scared. Very uncomfortable. Homosexuality wasn't an option for me. I hoped that if I ignored him he would move on to someone or something else. He didn't. The same thing happened a few more times that week. But only in the kitchen, when I was in line.

My first month in population had gone pretty smoothly—except for the guy with the crush on me. I spent seven hours a day on my job assignment at the sheet-metal welding shop, learning to weld. My first welding assignment was a hand-drawn blueprint by the tradesmen instructor—it called for welding two large rectangular iron frames with heavy mesh screening tacked to it. It took me most of a day to complete it, and the boss was pleased. I felt accomplishment in it.

When I wasn't at work, I tried to take advantage of every hour I could when we had access to the yard. I loved the sunshine—I'd missed it for nine months while I was in the closed quarters of the juvenile facility. With horseshoe pits, bocce ball courts, and plenty of grassy areas to lounge around, I loved being outside. Some guys sat in the grass playing cards, others gathered at "muscle beach" to work out and work on their tans. The "iron pile" was in the far corner of the prison yard, where free weights, dip, and pull-up bars were available. I spent a majority of my time there, and then I'd head over and relax at the beach.

One night I was out during evening yard, standing alone. I noticed the guy from the dining area, the one who blew kisses at me, was looking my way. My heart jumped into my throat. I didn't think much beyond an instinct to defend myself if he did anything to me. It was like survival mode kicked in.

He started walking toward me, wearing this grin as if I were his purpose. As he got close, he said, "You're one gorgeous motherf...!"

You know, I don't even remember swinging. The next thing I knew, my fist connected with his face, and he was reeling backward. He grabbed his nose, saw he had palms full of blood—he was stunned. So was I. My heart raced twice as fast now.

He lunged at me, but a group of his buddies restrained him and quickly pulled him away from me. One of his friends, a tiny little hunched-over guy named Shayeed, a guy who wore a Muslim kufi on his head, shouted to me, "You know what you gotta do now!" *No. I didn't.* "You gotta fight Nookie on the block."

Evening yard ended, and I returned to the housing unit with a hundred other men. My heart was pumping and my mind was racing. I was terrified. I stopped in front of my cell to look around, trying to spot the guy I was supposed to fight. I was in Cell 11. There were 33 on the range, so I was a third of the way down the hall. Long lines of guys were streaming in, passing by. The routine was that you come in, get to your cell, and wait for a CO to come get you for a shower. They'd take 10 or so at a time. But I was standing there thinking, *I can't go shower. I need to find and fight this guy.*

I felt a sting on my forehead. That's all I remember until I was trying to pick myself up off the floor.

I heard someone shout, "Damn, Nookie!" I was suddenly aware that several people surrounded me, asking, "Are you okay?"

I was dizzy but back on my feet. It felt like someone had poured warm liquid on me and it was running down my face. I reached up—it was blood. Lots of it.

Instinctively, I removed my t-shirt and held it to my head. Knowing I was badly hurt, I staggered to the front of the unit where the officers stood their post. One directed me to sit down on the steps. There was no pain. I had no idea what had occurred.

"What the hell happened to you?" an officer asked.

"I was horse-playing and fell into the bars," I said. He called other COs.

They all asked the same question. I gave them all the same answer. None of them were satisfied.

They took me to the hospital ward. A bunch of white-shirts—Commissioned Officers—showed up.

"What the hell happened? Who hit you?" they demanded. I stuck to my story. They got angry.

"We know you hit someone in the yard today. What did he say to you? Was it him?"

I kept denying it. "I don't know what you're talking about."

I really had no idea what had happened, or what would happen next, but I knew this: *I didn't want to be a snitch. Not in here. Not when you're here for the rest of your natural life.*

They stitched me up—three sutures here, four there. They were nursing knots on my head and bruises on my leg. As they worked on me, I noticed some crunching in my jaw whenever I bit down.

"Can you look at my jaw, Doc?" I asked. He did. He determined I had sustained a hairline fracture.

Turns out an officer had seen the altercation earlier in the yard, and was tracking after the both of us. They saw the assault on the unit. Nookie had taken a padlock, put it in a sock, and swung it at me. A couple of his buddies had grabbed my arms and locked them behind me. I got hit four or five times with the lock. They knew what happened—they just needed me to confirm the events. I wouldn't: "I told you—horseplay."

They wrapped me up and sent me to the RHU—Restricted Housing Unit, "the Hole"—while they continued their investigation. Ostensibly, I was going to the Hole for punching another inmate and for lying to officers investigating the assault. Justice.

The next morning they brought me back to the security office. Different day, but same questions. I gave them the same answers. They wanted me to give them names. They treated me as if I was the bad guy. They got right in my face and yelled at me. I could smell their breath—could have told them what they had eaten for breakfast.

One deputy laid pictures on the desk in front of me. "These are the guys!" he shouted.

"Nope," I said. "There were no guys. I fell on the bars." It went on for a long time.

Finally I'd had enough. "Look," I said, "You can shout at me all you want. I've got a life sentence. I've got to spend the rest of my life in here. I'm not telling on anyone. I fell on the bars. That's it."

They were furious. "Get him out of here!" one of them shouted.

One officer led me back to the Hole. On the way, we paused for a moment next to a cell—Nookie's cell. He was sitting on the edge of his bed.

"Hey man," he called to me. "I'm sorry. It went too far. As far as I'm concerned, it's over."

Whether he was saying that because he was genuinely sorry or because he was hoping I wouldn't tell on him, I don't know. Either way, I was ready to move on.

So there I sat, in the Hole—unable to eat. When they realized I couldn't chew anything, they moved me to the hospital unit. I'd get to do my 30 days of isolation in the hospital—an awesome upgrade compared to the Hole! In fact, while I was in there, I lined it up: when I got out of isolation, I'd get a job at the hospital unit.

I was back in general population just a few days when I looked up to see a couple of Nookie's boys coming my way. *Here we go again.*

I stood up, prepared for something—I didn't know what—to happen. Shayeed, the little guy wearing a little hat, walked right up close to me. "As far as we're concerned, you're a cool white boy and you'll never have any problems with us. Cool?"

I nodded.

Turns out the administration had transferred Nookie, but before he left he let his buddies know that I never told on him. They knew I kept my mouth shut, and they respected that.

And what I found out later? Nookie was a golden-glove champion! Had it come down to a fight, he'd have beaten the heck out of me! I probably faired much better with the lock in a sock to my head.

CHAPTER 5

DARKNESS, LIES, AND GLIMMERS OF LIGHT

Those prison stories Bobby had told me—stories of the boxing matches he'd won, the weight-training he'd done, the stories of men dressing up like women—it all sounded so adventurous and fascinating compared to my gloomy teen home life. But in reality, prison life is a grind.

I'd been at Camp Hill for three months. I guess I was flexing my prison muscles—sort of like an adolescent might stand up to a parent for the first time hoping to demonstrate "I'm a grown-up, now." Whatever you call it, it became a lesson: if you look for trouble, you'll find it.

"Turn that radio off, McGuire!" came a command from the night shift officer, making his rounds. "You hear me? Turn it off!"

I lay still in my bunk, ignoring the man standing just outside the bars of my cell.

Power was turned off in our cells at 10PM on weekdays, but my radio operated on batteries—and I was in a defiant frame of mind. He shined his flashlight into my eyes. "Let's go, McGuire! Turn it off!"

He couldn't do anything. He wasn't going to come in and turn it off himself. I wasn't moving. I felt powerful.

He tapped his flashlight a few times on the bars of my cell. He turned it off and on a few times in my face. He got louder, "Now, McGuire!"

"Go f... yourself!" I shouted. I heard snickering up and down the range.

The officer turned his flashlight up to the name plate on my cell, scratched a couple notes on a pad in his pocket, and walked away. I felt like I'd accomplished something great. It was a contest of wills, and I'd won! I smiled ear to ear.

Music was a great distraction for me. During the long evenings, tunes made the time pass. Wings, maybe some Queen with a little luck, Meatloaf's *Two out of Three Ain't Bad*—it took me out of the box. *Who were they to tell me to turn it off?* I eventually fell asleep to the music.

Doors sliding, open and closed, was like an alarm clock on the range. Morning had come. I rolled over and noticed a yellow form on the floor of my cell. I leapt out of bed and grabbed it—a JBC-141 form, Inmate Misconduct Report. I read the night shift officer's incident report. It stated that while he was making his rounds he heard a loud radio playing from Cell 23, and he ordered me to turn it off. "Refusing to obey my order, Inmate McGuire used profanity toward this officer."

Along with the misconduct form was a response form for me to fill out and submit, because I'd been ordered to report to the Hearing Examiner the next day. I tossed the response form aside—the officer's take pretty much summed it up.

I lost privileges for a week. In the long run, muscle-flexing endeavors don't add up the way you'd hope.

I decided to put my machismo into studying for the GED test.

School had been a real challenge for me. I didn't do too bad with math, but English, history, and other subjects were a real struggle. With no accountability at home, it was easy for me to ignore my homework. I failed to turn in a lot of assignments, or I'd hurriedly complete something at the last moment, and my grades reflected it. On test days I'd cringe, not knowing the answers and hoping for some multiple choice questions so at least I'd have options upon which to guess.

In prison I realized that I had potential to do well—to get a diploma—if I applied myself to the coursework. I determined to do it. My grind included working seven hours a day—for a whopping 10 cents an hour—going to school in the late afternoons to study for the GED, and then filling every other waking hour with power-lifting in the yard.

I was also getting high.

You'd think drugs wouldn't make their way into prison. But surprise. Inmates have visitors smuggle in small quantities of weed—any drugs, really—with relative ease. Sometimes an inmate would throw the stash into a wastebasket, knowing that another prisoner would be on trash detail later that night with opportunity to fish it out and carry it back to the cell block. Sometimes deliveries came packed in balloons so an inmate could swallow them, pass through the strip search returning to population, and then ... wait for nature to take its course.

I did that once. Not a pleasant experience. My brother Mike came to visit and tossed a bag of Doritos on the table in front of me.

"Thanks, but I'm not hungry," I said, sliding the bag back to him.

"You're going to want to eat those," he said, sliding it back. I looked inside and saw four or five balloons.

In the visitation area, there is an officer on a watch platform. But there are a lot of people, vending machines, microwave ovens, people eating snacks together—they can't catch everything. As inconspicuously as I could, I started eating. I managed to swallow the balloons and nervously went back to my cell. There I drank some soapy water to make myself throw-up. A couple balloons came back up. I had to wait for the others—eventually digging them out of the toilet. I wouldn't be doing any more of that!...

I got deeper into weed with a buddy whose girlfriend snuck it in to him.

Working as a hospital orderly at that time, I often walked by the hallway to the visiting room during my shift. My buddy saw me from the visiting area one day, and we hatched a plan. He said, "Next time I see you, I'll throw something down the hall." So he did. I pocketed it and took it back to the cell. We split it up, rolled some joints, and we were in business. The plan was to sell some and smoke the rest. But just as quick, I got careless. I got busted.

It happened in the education room as I was studying for my GED one day. I had about 20 joints in an envelope in my pocket—at the ready, to sell, trade, or barter. When I got up to leave the room, an officer stopped me.

"Everyone, line up for a pat-down," he said.

He patted me, felt something in my pocket and asked, "What's that right there?" He pulled out the envelope.

"It's just an empty envelope," I said.

He opened it. "Come with me."

I tried to explain that it wasn't my coat—I must have picked someone else's up by mistake.

They weren't buying my lies, of course.

I was sent to solitary confinement for 45 days. Back in the Hole. The cells in solitary housing are empty except for an old, dirty, thin mattress on a metal bed frame and a stark toilet. It's by design—they're not meant to be comfortable. They're supposed to be intimidating. You are left alone with your thoughts and imagination—not exactly the best company. You were lucky if you could request a library book or find someone to give you a newspaper. If you got your hands on a newspaper, you'd read every story and every advertisement on every page—probably several times.

It's just you in that tiny cell, hour after hour. The highlights of the experience are that they take you out to shower three times a week. You are also permitted one hour of exercise, five times a week, in a small caged-in area. You look forward to those moments because any opportunity to be free of that tiny concrete cell was a big relief.

My experience in solitary confinement assured me that it wasn't just another part of the prison like some of guys who had been there said. There may have been 150 or so inmates isolated down there. Some of the COs, out of sheer boredom, no doubt, created tension among the inmates by intentionally stirring things up. If the inmates were quiet, officers might make mention of somebody's crimes, or say something about their past that could be picked up and talked about. It made for constant fear and tension. You didn't want to be the next topic.

There is a saying about the Hole: "Up all night. Sleep all day." I didn't understand it until I was there. Your first few days you just about go mad with boredom. There is nothing to occupy your mind. To combat the monotony, you try to sleep as much as possible, thus the "Sleep all day."

By nightfall, when it's dark, you are wide awake and listening in on the other inmates' discussions nearby. It's possible to get to know a lot about the guys around you even without ever seeing what they look like.

Nights can be unbearable in the Hole. If the night officers don't make their proper 30-minute rounds enforcing the rules, inmates get loud, shouting to others 10 or 15 cells away. When a bunch of guys get going, they compete with one another to be heard. It's impossible to sleep—"Up all night."

I made a concerted effort at first to exhaust myself during the day—working out several times, even pacing the short distance around my cell for hours at a time, hoping to be tired enough to sleep at night. It really was no use—the noise level was intolerable.

Eventually I stopped fighting it and joined the flow of the unit. I'd listen in, re-read any newspapers I'd gotten, pace some more, altering my body clock until things quieted down. Things were usually quietest between 5AM and 1PM. Solitary confinement's clock was the opposite of that in general population.

Emotionally, it was a very dark experience. I felt really bad about getting caught and losing what privileges I had earned in population. Being isolated in the Hole for weeks causes you to appreciate what little you do have all the more. Visits, for instance. You lose visitation privileges in the Hole.

I knew my brother was planning to come visit me. I quickly sent word to him about my circumstances so he wouldn't waste a trip. I was embarrassed. In my letter I asked him not to tell anyone—especially my mom and step-dad—what I'd done.

A week or so had gone by when they delivered a letter to me—it was addressed from Michigan, from Kathy McGuire, a name I didn't know. Her letter began with an apology: "Dear Gene, I apologize for opening the personal note you sent to your brother. The truth is that I was so very curious how a letter you addressed to a McGuire in Scranton, Pennsylvania, wound up in our mailbox in Livonia, Michigan. I think it might be the hand of God."

My brother never received the letter I sent him. This lady did.

Kathy went on to introduce herself—she was a pastor's wife and a mother. She explained that as she read my letter, she "felt compelled to write back and to share the love of God" with me. She didn't think it a coincidence that my letter had found itself so far out of the way. She went on and on about how she believed God had plans for me, in spite of my situation.

Looking back, I don't think the spiritual tone of her letter really made much of an impression on me. I was certainly surprised that my letter had traveled two states in the wrong direction but would easily have attributed that to a flawed U.S. postal system before branding it an act of God. But the warmth of her tone and the fact that she'd included pictures of her family did touch me. Here was a stranger, demonstrating some kindness and care for me—someone she'd never met, didn't know, and had only happened upon by chance. Astounding.

Kathy and her husband wrote to me pretty much weekly for the next year. Each letter spoke of God's love, God's forgiveness, and God's plan. It wasn't until years later that I'd look back on this entire episode as a means of God's voice calling out to my wayward heart.

If I did have any God thoughts during that time—while I was in the Hole, especially—they were along the lines of bargaining with Him: "Okay, God, if you get me out of here, I'll never get high again!"

I don't guess I gave God the credit when my 45 days in the Hole were cut short—they let me out after only 30.

And my first thought? *Pot!*

My cell—I wondered if they'd found the stash I had hidden back in my cell. They'd taken my envelope of 20 joints when I got caught, but I had another 20 or more concealed in my mattress. I wondered if they'd tossed my cell and found it.

Once I was back to my mattress, I discovered the dope was safe—and I was getting high again within moments of being sprung. So much for my "I'll never do it again" religious confession and the admonitions of my well-wishing, mail-poaching, Christian pen-pals from Michigan.

I got back to my general population routine, work and working out. But because I'd been sent to solitary confinement, I was removed from school and the GED preparation classes. I'd have to start over from the beginning. And start over I did—several more months of classes and study.

But the day for me to take the GED finally arrived. I was nervous. I was 20 years old by then, in prison since I was 18, incarcerated since I was 17—it was time for me to have a high-school-equivalency diploma.

I was so happy to hear that I passed! And I felt a real sense of accomplishment. I'd followed through.

Camp Hill threw a grand celebration. Graduates were allowed to invite guests. My mom and my sister, Mary, made the trip. I had a cap and gown. Mom and Mary were dressed up. We had cake and juice to celebrate and time to take pictures. It wasn't the typical high school graduation that moms look forward to cherishing with their kids, but this was a special day.

My earliest school memories are of Immaculate Conception Grade School in West Pittston, PA. Actually, my most vivid memories are of nuns—intimidating nuns, scary nuns. Snapping at you for every little thing, hiding beneath their long flowing holy habits—essentially a big black robe, a scapular apron, and a white coif on their heads—covering all but their scowling faces. It made for sheer terror to my five-, six- and seven-year-old eyes. Kindergarten through second grade—and lucky me, I got to repeat second grade—it was my own personal education purgatory.

I recall a few happier things ... cookies and juice in Sunday School classes, first communion ... and that stuff wasn't so bad. But the confessional—by far—was most terrifying. They forced you to step inside a closet and speak to a priest, to tell him all the things you'd done wrong. I could see his face through a little latticed opening. I really don't remember what he said to me, but I could smell his breath—it was desperately-needed-a-breath-mint bad.

Confess my sins? I had no idea what to tell the man. Sometimes I just made stuff up so I'd have something to say. It was a traumatic experience for a kid, and void of any meaning for me.

I didn't get Catholicism. I remember it was important to my dad to teach me to pray the rosary, to recite the *Our Father* and *Hail Mary*. It just never connected for me. It was empty ritual.

I was 7 when my parents divorced. One good thing about this change in our life circumstances was that it meant the end of our Catholic school elementary education. Mom wanted us to continue in the church, but we moved to Toms River, NJ, and parochial school was out the question for our new economic realities. *Whew!*

Still desiring her children have some spiritual influence in their lives, Mom found a Protestant Sunday School class we could attend in our new neighborhood. I didn't get Protestantism, either.

The class met in some little house-trailer sort of dwelling, I remember it was about a block from the beach. It felt corny to me—listening to Bible stories and singing songs. They did serve up the familiar cookies and juice—I guess Catholics and Protestants had that much in common.

Mom would drop us off—me, Mike, and Mary—and she'd leave. After the first couple of times, Mike and I figured out that we could hit the cookies and juice, and then seize an opportune moment to slip out a side door when no one was looking to walk down to the beach. Stellar childcare ... they never missed us!

Mike was around 10, I was 8 or so. It became our routine. Years later, Mary called us on it: "You guys left me there!" I suppose we weren't the most caring older brothers.

When Mom decided to move us back to Pennsylvania—after the failed relationship with the womanizer—she gave up altogether on trying to get us to church. That was fine with me. It would be a few years before I'd bump into Christianity again.

Bill was my best friend through junior high and high school. His was a Christian home. He wasn't too deeply rooted in faith himself, but he did know a lot about it and the Bible. Looking back, he probably wasn't any different from other churchgoing teens at that time; his was more a knowledge about Christianity rather than a genuine relationship with its Deity.

I remember Bill showing me some things in the Bible he'd learned. It was cool stuff for us kids—a guy named Methuselah who lived 969 years, a guy named Noah who lived more than 900. Now those guys were old! That stuff was fun to read about, to talk about, to ponder. He wasn't trying to convince me to believe anything—I'm not even really sure what he believed at that point in his life—we were just friends, talking.

Bill's mom, however, was a different story. One night we were hanging out at his house while she made us some steak hoagies. "Gene, how would you boys like to come with me to church tonight?" I must have giggled out loud. I got a swift kick in the leg beneath the table, and Bill gave me a stern look that warned this wasn't a laughing matter to her.

I don't suppose I found her offer to go to church amusing. It was just that Bill and I had planned to meet up with some girls at the mall that night. *Let's see ... girls or church?* I politely declined. When she left, Bill told me his mom was a born-again Christian. That may have been the first time I heard that term, *born-again*.

My next brush with Christianity came in a very pretty package—named Kim. This girl always wore dresses to school. Her hair was always nicely styled. She was beautiful. She smelled great. And she was really nice. I took a liking to her the first time I saw her.

My first inkling that she was a religious girl came when we were trying to set up a double date—me and Kim with Bill and his girlfriend Tammy. Tammy was a couple years older than us and had a driver's license with access to a car. We planned a date to a drive-in movie for a Friday night.

Kim spoke up. "We're Christians. My parents will never allow me to go to a drive-in with a boy."

"No worries," I told her. "We'll lie." We'd tell her parents we were going to the Dietrich Theatre in Tunkhannock—a regular sit-in-rows-of-chairs-surrounded-by-other-people theatre, much safer for a young lady of virtue than the drive-in.

The next Monday she came to school and told me she was grounded—her parents had somehow figured out that we lied, and that we'd gone to the drive-in. That wasn't the end of our relationship, however. Jail would be.

Kim wrote to me after I was arrested. During my first month or two in juvenile detention, we exchanged a few letters—they were certainly welcome because I couldn't receive any visitors outside of my immediate family while there. In her letters, Kim tried to share the Gospel with me. She assured me that if I would just believe in Jesus He would forgive my sins. I didn't get it. I didn't care to. I just knew I didn't want her to stop writing.

But stop she did—and that was the end of us. I am certain Kim's Christian parents had higher hopes for their daughter than the kid who dragged her off to a drive-in movie ... and then graduated to a murder sentence.

After earning my GED, I spent the next few years working a 6AM-to-2PM shift every day in the infirmary. I'd help with patients who were temporarily housed in the unit; some came in with broken bones from sports injuries, others who were sick. I'd feed them and care for them throughout the day. Sometimes we'd have patients who were seriously ill and required around-the-clock care. I enjoyed the work.

The guy who hired me was Harold. He had served as a medic in the Navy for years before coming into Corrections. He was married to Phyllis, who worked in Administration—they were two wonderful people ... and, as it turned out, devout Christians.

Harold never spoke about his faith with me, but he was a testimony—

the way he treated me, the way he lived his life. It was attractive. He didn't drink. He didn't cuss. He was a family man—his love for his wife and their two daughters was very evident. It's almost understandable, with thousands of prisoners, that staff would treat inmates like numbers. It stands out, like night and day, when a staff member really cares. Harold did.

Funny story. Once, not long after I started working in the infirmary, I called my brother, Mike, and asked him to send me a sweatshirt and sweatpants to work out in. It was something I couldn't pick up inside but really needed. He said he'd take care of it. Pretty soon a package arrived in the property room. I opened it up—the sweatsuit was pink! He'd sent me a girl's sweatsuit!

I called him up and was like, "What the...?!"

And he apologized. "Sorry. I just ordered it. I didn't look at it." He told me to send it back—pretty much impossible for me from prison.

I was sharing my pink dilemma with Harold later that day. He laughed. I had to laugh, too.

Then he said, "Hey Gene, how about this?" He explained that he had daughters. They'd love the pink sweatsuit. He could buy me a new sweatsuit—one made for a man—and trade with me. I was thrilled.

That's the kind of guy he was.

As the years went on, we started getting more and more psychiatric patients in the infirmary. The state of Pennsylvania began closing state-run mental facilities, and the prison system was being used to house displaced patients. I was doing suicide watches—walk by every 15 minutes to ask, "Are you still alive?"

And that's when my job in the infirmary ceased to be fun. I did that for about a year and a half more, and I'd had enough. Harold suggested maybe

I might be happier working in the medical administration office—where his wife worked.

I enjoyed working for Phyllis and Joyce there. They were wonderful ladies—genuine and caring. One of the perks I enjoyed was when, every now and then, they'd bring me in some fast food from Hardees. Both were Christians, though Joyce was more vocal about her beliefs. She'd tell me about her church and encourage me to attend some of the religious services offered in the prison. "You'll like it," she promised. I couldn't see how.

There was no shortage of religious meetings inmates could participate in, but I really had no interest. Another inmate convinced me to try out the Catholic service with him—not for the faith, mind you, but for the wine.

"Holy communion," he said. "They pass around a cup of wine. They sip. We gulp!"

So we'd get high and then go to church—to have some wine. We'd say to Father Beamon, "Hey, Father, this cup is empty. You need to fill it up again!"

We didn't become regular attenders—you had to sort of weigh whether it was worth sitting through the long, boring mass for a gulp of wine. But every now and again, it was something to do.

In 1981, I got the news that my biological father died of cirrhosis of the liver. All those years of drinking, the healthy tissue in his liver had putrefied to the point of shutting down. The prison administration made it possible for me to attend his funeral.

It's a big drawn-out ordeal to move a prisoner. I was processed out to a couple of officers—in this case, the same ones who had brought me to Camp Hill a few years earlier. They transported me to the local county jail for an overnight stay. It was really an old dungeon at the time. The next morning, the officers returned and escorted me, in handcuffs and shackles, by car, but took them off when we arrived for the viewing and funeral so I wouldn't be a distraction.

Stacy was her name—the beautiful young lady who sat down next to me and introduced herself as my step-sister. Dad had remarried a year or so earlier. I'd only met her once before they were married—Dad brought her on a visit—his last visit to see me. Stacy told me they'd been happy, her mom and my dad, in the short time they had together. She held my hand and gently rubbed it during the entire service.

She looked deeply into my eyes. "He really loved you," she said. "I tried to talk with him about Jesus there at the end."

I had no idea what any of that meant, or why she chose to share it with me—but I did like her holding my hand. While she was gently caressing my hand, looking at me like that, she could have said just about anything and I'd have nodded along in agreement.

On the way back to Camp Hill, I couldn't get her out of my mind.

I quickly wrote a letter to my dad's widow—expressed my condolences and regrets that I hadn't gotten to know her better, and then I asked about Stacy. They both came to visit me.

The best way to sum it up is like this: I was very interested in Stacy; she was only interested in my soul.

She gave me a Bible with all sorts of highlighted passages in it. I wasn't big on reading in general and hadn't been interested in the Bible any further than Bill and my teenage conversations about old Noah and Methuselah, but I spent some time flipping through her highlights. 1 Corinthians 13 was all about love—I loved the fact that she highlighted that! And Acts 2, the rushing wind, the tongues of fire, the supernatural phenomena that overwhelmed the crowd—I found it engaging.

Stacy wrote me long letters—like 20 pages long. Most of those were filled with spiritual stuff, Bible stuff, encouragement for me to believe. I wanted this to be about me and Stacy. She was clearly making it about me and Jesus.

There was one fellow inmate who stood out among all the others where Jesus was concerned—a guy named Warner, who we called "Big Moses."

Warner was different than the other churchgoing guys in my mind, because he was genuine, through and through. Yes, he was a ham—he'd get up early every morning and shout, "Get up, you convicts, and praise the Lord! This is the day the Lord has made! Rise up! Rejoice and be glad in it!"

And everyone down the range would shout, "Shut up, Moses! It's too damn early!"

But he was authentic, the real deal. The way he treated others, his gentleness in the face of threats, his calm in the face of stressful circumstances, I knew that this guy believed what he was preaching. He lived his creed.

I asked Warner to look at the letters Stacy sent me. I guess I was hoping he'd read between the lines and tell me, "Man, this girl is into you, Gene." Instead, what he did was confirm for me, "She's telling you the truth; that's some good advice she's giving you about Jesus."

After a while, Stacy and I quit writing. She wasn't coming around to love. I wasn't coming around to faith. But there was this: I did pick up that Bible she'd given me every now and again, re-read those highlighted passages. They held my interest.

And Warner's morning routine may have started to feel a little different to me, too...

Great is Thy faithfulness!
Great is Thy faithfulness!
Morning by morning new mercies I see.
All I have needed Thy hand hath provided;

Great is Thy faithfulness, Lord, unto me!

He'd finish a chorus and then shout, "Sing with me, men!"

And many voices would erupt in unison, "Come on, Moses! It's too damn early!"

He'd laugh ... and sing all the louder.

1976 - Me, Dad and his girlfriend

1977 - Sophomore at Tunkhannock HS. Go Tigers!

1977 - At my brother Michael's Wedding. Left to right: Debbie, Michael, me, Dad and Mary

July 1977 - Transported to the courthouse for a hearing. That's deputy Truesdale on the left, a friend of my mom's and a caring man.

July 1977 - My cousin Bobby arriving at the courthouse for the same hearing. This would be the first time I saw him since I left New York City. That's a pretty representative picture of Bobby—cool, calm, looking right into the camera.

July 1977 - My stepbrother Sid arriving for the same hearing. Notice he is not in handcuffs or shackles. He arrived that day believing he was a witness. He'd be arrested before the day ended, a co-defendant.

1979 - Receiving my GED at Camp Hill.

June 1989 - Newspaper clipping of my visit with Senators John Heinz and Arlen Specter discussing prison overcrowding. Left to right: Lamont, Senator Heinz, Senator Specter, me, Frank.

1983 - At SCI Camp Hill with my sister in law Debbie and my niece Shannon.

1996 - My brother Mike and his second wife Lisa visiting me at SCI Rockview.

2001 - Chaplain Reitz (glasses), Warner and me, baptizing Will, aka Surf at SCI Rockview. Will, a lifer, continues to be one of the most fruitful disciples I have ever invested in.

2004 - Rockview Lifer's Basketball Team.

2004 - Surrounding our pastor, Chaplain Reitz (sweater) before a service.

2005 - Visiting Room photo with Bill and Karen Nast, and their daughters Emily and Jordyn.

2007 - Preparing for Worship before Baptism Service. Me, Will and Warner

2007 - Conclusion of our Mission Week services, with guys whose lives I had the privilege of investing in.

2007 - Ministry leaders at Rockview, from left: Warner (Big Moses), Suave, me, Pastor Reitz, Orlando and Will (Surf).

2008 - Conducting the service and offering instructions to those coming to the altar.

Pastors Reitz and White are in the tank, and I'm sharing on the meaning and importance of baptism.

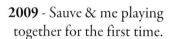

2007 - Spending time with ministry leaders at Rockview.

2008 - Getting ready for an evening worship service. Bryan (with his arm around me) and the guys, SCI Rockview Chapel

2009 - Sauve & me playing together for the first time.

April 3, 2012 - Freedom!

April 3, 2012 - Me and my sister Mary.

April 3, 2012 - Moments after my release from the Wyoming County Court House. My sister Mary waited with me for 34 years nine months and 15 days for this incredible day.

April 3, 2012 - Release day with nephew Mark.

April 3, 2012 - Moments after my release with Bill Nast.

April 3, 2012 - Standing outside the Court House, listening to my Attorney Robert Buttner's encouraging words after my release while family and friends listen in.

April 4, 2012 - With Jim Neary, Deputy Director of Probation, at Mary's House, the day after my release.

April 29, 2012 - My first day in Texas after my release. With the Titus and Lozano family. Rob Meier (far right) flew me down 1st class.

April 8, 2012 - Preparing to speak at Grace & Glory Outreach Sunday, five days after my release.

April 29, 2012 - My first day in Texas with Pastor Larry and Devi Titus.

CHAPTER 6

THAT'S LIFE BEHIND BARS

I worked with Joyce and Phyllis in the medical administration office for a year or so before moving on. It was in 1983 that I got a job in the commissary, easily the most desirable job for inmates, as it came with a better wage—20 cents an hour—and a number of other perks. Often, at the end of a week, the supervisor would reward workers with commissary items, a few packs of cigarettes, prison-trading commodity gold, or the equivalent. If the inventory was within a hundred bucks of balancing at the end of a month, there were even more perks.

The commissary job was meaningful, too, in that an inmate had to be recognized as trustworthy to work there. They couldn't have just anyone in there to steal or try to leverage their position. It felt good to me that I was trusted.

The work itself was really easy. You'd open your window and inmates would line up to shop for items like toiletries, snacks, and smokes. They'd have to present a commissary sheet, properly filled out. Our job was to fill their orders—going and pulling the various items from the shelves and charging their accounts.

It got tough when an inmate would present a lengthy list and I would have to explain they didn't have enough money in their account to pay for it. It happened often and could get pretty unpleasant. Guys would argue that their family members or friends had sent in money. All we could do was go by what was there on the books. Sometimes they'd blame us—suggesting we were lying or had stolen their funds. Still, the job was a good one to have.

One morning, we arrived to find a section of the ceiling had fallen down, right over the boss's desk. Hunks of block and plaster littered his desktop, and a layer of dust covered everything. None of us were surprised. The old prison had stood for a hundred or so years and was showing her age—failures and flaws like this were a regular occurrence. One day it was the plumbing, next day the electric. For maintenance staff, the old facility was a repair-du-jour for sure.

We all pitched in to sweep and mop up the mess, hurrying so we could open our windows on time. Around lunch the boss got a call. They wanted to know if he noticed anything missing from the inventory. My boss looked more closely at the ceiling, eventually climbing up onto his desk and pushing at it. A few more pieces pulled loose. He realized it wasn't the usual old facility rot—someone had done this deliberately. Just then, another block fell to the floor with a thud, and an officer stuck his head down into the room from above.

"Well I'll be damned!" he said. "These idiots broke into the commissary!"

In a flash, the shift Captain and several Lieutenants raced in, stood looking up through the hole in the ceiling, and surveyed the scene. My boss looked dazed—incredulous. How could this have happened? The officers figured out that the men in Cell Block E, directly above, had manipulated a lock, and had somehow carved their way down through. I'd seen movies—*Escape from Alcatraz*, for instance. I wasn't surprised. It was actually pretty impressive.

They'd only figured it out because an officer making his rounds that morning had noticed an inordinate amount of commissary items on inmates' shelves. One guy had a hundred bars of Irish Spring soap, another had three dozen bottles of Suave shampoo, still another had piles of cookies and bags of coffee. "It was like they were displaying it for guys to see," he said.

A search was conducted on the block above us. Some of the items were recovered and returned. Others had been trashed or distributed. Inmates who had more than $50 worth of commissary items in their cells—the allowable limit for one person—were given a misconduct. They launched an investigation, and those deemed responsible for the break-in were given 60 days in the Hole and forced to make restitution until all the money was recouped.

Undoubtedly, a number of guys who had done nothing wrong paid a price that day, as commissary items that were rightfully theirs were confiscated, too. Such is life behind bars.

Hearing your name and number called out over the PA system for a visit was a wonderful reprieve from the prison grind. It was pretty much the best feeling you'd have during a day—someone was there to see you! It didn't matter that you wouldn't know who it was until you walked into the visiting room, the excitement that someone from the outside world was waiting was an absolute highlight. As an inmate, the prison system isolates you from society; a visitor from the outside makes you forget that part of your punishment, if even for just a few moments.

Receiving a visitor is a process, too—no matter where you are in the institution, at your job or out in the yard, you have to report back to your unit before proceeding to the visit. Your Sergeant calls to confirm, and then you are sent to the visiting room. The irony? Every inmate rushes to get back, hurrying to make that visit, but the routine is always the same: waiting on the Sergeant to make the call, waiting to have the visit confirmed, waiting to be searched, waiting to change, waiting for gates to open. It can be maddening.

And it isn't a perfect system. On one occasion I heard my name called while I was out in the yard. I raced back to my cell, put on some deodorant, brushed my teeth and hair, then raced into the process I described—waiting at every turn. When I got through the pre-visit strip search and changed into the brown jumpsuit, I finally stepped into the visiting room ... and didn't see a single familiar face.

I thought perhaps my visitor had stepped into the restroom. I waited for a few moments. A lot of people were looking at me now, wondering why I was just standing there.

The officer at the desk called me over and asked, "What are you doing?"

"I don't know," I said. "They called me out for a visit."

He checked his list. "No Gene McGuire, here." It was a mistake. There was no one there to see me.

Heading back, I was so disappointed. All that excitement—then nothing. Then it hit me that somewhere there was an inmate who was having to wait that much longer for *his* visit, might even run out of visiting hours before they got it straightened out. It was just wrong.

Again, life behind bars.

When I was initially in the juvenile facility, only my parents could come visit. My dad came once. They sat us in a hallway—he was drunk. *Nothing has changed.*

He spoke up. "You know, I might have expected this from your brothers, from Chuckie or Mike. But not you."

I didn't know what that meant. *Was he saying he cared more about me? Had higher hopes for me? Was more disappointed in me?* I didn't have an answer for him.

"Thanks for coming." It would be years until I'd see him again, just a few months before his passing.

My mom came to see me once a month or so when I was in juvie. After they sentenced me and sent me to Camp Hill, she came a couple times a year. Her early visits were tough. I was so glad to see her, but many times she'd show up drunk or high on prescription painkillers. It was so obvious—she'd slur her words and often repeat herself without realizing it. On those occasions, I'd sit there just watching the clock, wishing the visit would end.

Sometimes she'd bring my sister with her. Those visits were highlights. I loved seeing Mary. And when Mary got married and had two children of her own, she'd bring my niece and nephew with her, so they would know their Uncle Gene as they were growing up. Man, that was awesome. I was so proud of them—those visits were the best of all.

A few of my friends from high school came to visit me early on, but once they got to be college age and started into their adult lives, they were too busy—life got in the way. We kept in touch through letters.

Come to think of it, that's one lesson I remember my dad offering me. He'd told me, "If you want letters, you've got to write them." So I wrote to anyone and everyone. If someone wrote back to me, I'd reply immediately, the same day I received theirs. The old man was right. It worked. Letters were a lifeline.

Visits from family and friends from back home became rare. The two-and-a-half-hour drive each way made for a long day for anyone wanting to come. I understood. I began reaching out to the guys I served time with, any of them with sisters or friends to lend. I sent out a lot of letters hoping to connect with somebody—to get a visit out of it.

It worked.

Having a pretty girl come to visit became a validation for me—I was a guy, a girl cared about me, I mattered to someone. It felt great. It was like an addiction of sorts—find and engage a girl in a relationship. A hug, a kiss, a little hand-holding with a pretty girl was an oh-so-welcome break from prison reality. Some guys would even try to sneak into the waiting area restroom to steal a moment or two "behind closed doors" with their girls. I always wanted to—never had the nerve. But these visits I shared with girls were heart candy enough for me. And there were several over the years.

Cathy was a long-blonde-haired beauty with a wonderful smile. She was a fellow inmate's sister—it so happened we had visits at the same time one day and I spotted her. I asked if I could write her, and that's how it started.

I took a real liking to her. I longed for her visits. She usually wore form-fitting jeans. You bet I noticed.

One day when Cathy visited, she kept her beautiful smile hidden. I noticed her holding a hand up in front of her mouth as she spoke. Something was up. So I asked.

She tried to say nothing was wrong, but that was obviously not true. Eventually she told me the story.

She was at a party and things got out of hand. The police were called— she got into an altercation with an officer who punched her in the mouth. I reached over and lowered her hand. Sure enough—front and center—a missing tooth! What a difference it made in her smile. I tried so hard not to giggle.

She got her tooth fixed eventually. And we visited for probably a year or so before I met another girl. Moving on....

This new young lady had just gone through a failed marriage. I felt like a hero in her life, the new guy replacing the old guy. We went on about a year or so, too. Then one day she said something that really took me aback: "It's so cool that you're locked in prison, because I have a boyfriend available whenever I want, but you can't run around and cheat on me."

It was obvious, she didn't care for me the way I had begun caring about her. It was a real turn-off.

In my head and in my heart, I started to lose interest in our relationship that day. I began to make excuses why I couldn't visit with her. I even refused to go out to the visiting room one day when she came, to avoid seeing her. I felt bad—and guys dogged me about that for a long time.

Another girl and I grew pretty close. She worked as an intern in the prison medical office. When she finished her internship, I asked if I could have her address and phone number to stay in touch. She was going home to work for her dad's insurance company, and they lived close to the prison. She could visit often—and she did. She was the sweetest girl. And she loved to visit me. Of course, I loved the companionship and having someone to visit with, write, and talk to on the telephone.

One day she told me she'd had a talk with her father and told him she was "willing to wait for me" to get out of prison. I was surprised. Although I loved our relationship, I wasn't *in* love with her. I felt bad—like she had designs on us that wouldn't, or couldn't, be. Hearing her express how she felt made me uncomfortable. I had to let her know I couldn't be committed to her, and that I didn't want her committed to waiting for me. It just wouldn't work. Thankfully, that didn't end our relationship—we continued to correspond as friends.

A little more time passed, and—you guessed it—I met another young lady through an outside volunteer program at the prison.

Kelli had a boyfriend. But she assured me he didn't mind our seeing each other as long as we didn't hug. We agreed; we would mind our relationship, keep a healthy boundary, and just be friends.

Oh, but hug we did. Whenever I'd step into the visiting room to meet her, Kelli jumped out of her chair and ran to meet me, throwing herself into my arms. She'd squeeze the snot out of me! I squeezed back. And I loved it! Everyone who saw us was certain we were a romantic couple. Nope. Just friends.

Looking back on those years I realize I was a real mess where self-worth was concerned. A lot of the guys in prison use the girls who visit them—talk them into smuggling in drugs or other contraband, or talk them into depositing money into their accounts. I never did that. Never. But I was using these girls all the same, for my happiness, to make me feel better about myself.

I'd come to an awakening on this eventually...

But turning back to my mom again ... something amazing happened in her life. One day she came to visit me—must have been in 1984 or '85 I think—and it was overwhelmingly evident there was a night and day difference.

"I'm a Christian, Gene," she said.

Did I hear her right?

"I gave my life to Jesus Christ!"

I was happy for her, but probably a little skeptical. Happy that she'd found something to make life add up for her—skeptical because years of my experience with her argued *This can't be for real.* But what I was seeing couldn't be denied. She looked great!

She was sober, clean, lucid, loving ... the mom I'd always wanted. From that day forward, visits with Mom were amazing. I realized how much I loved her—how much I always had. And now I could be proud of her, too. Whereas before I would be embarrassed of her, I now found myself wanting to tell others, "Hey! Everybody! This is my mom!"

·————⋟⊷●⊶⋞————·

"What are you doing, man?"

His words pierced through a cloud of smoke, interrupting my escape from reality. I'd been lying on my bunk, puffing on a joint, getting baked.

I looked up to see Warner staring through the bars of my cell. He had earned favor with the officers on the cell block, and had a sort of standing permission to walk around and talk to guys at will.

There he stood, engaging me, "Don't you even care who might walk up on you?"

I guess it was out of respect for him—since he was one of the genuinely good guys—I sat up and put out my joint.

"Man, I could have been an officer making rounds. You would've been busted. Don't you get it, man? Don't you care?"

"I'm not worried about it," was all I could think to say. I had actually sunken to that level—the level of indifference—and I really didn't think I'd get caught.

Warner stared at me. It was probably only a matter of seconds, but it felt longer—real long, uncomfortably long. I wondered what he was thinking. I was actually feeling a little embarrassed.

"Gene, I was just reading in Lamentations this morning," he finally spoke. "It's a book that was written by the prophet Jeremiah. You ever heard of it?"

He didn't wait for me to answer. "You know what it says? 'It is of the Lord's mercies that we are not consumed, because his compassions fail not. They are new every morning: great is thy faithfulness.'"

His face was suddenly overtaken by an ear-to-ear smile. It was like his soul responded to his own words—they caught him afresh—he began to bounce on his toes at the thought of what he was sharing.

"It's real, Gene. It's truth, man. New mercies. Every morning. You hear me?"

Warner spun to leave, humming, and then singing, "Great is Thy faithfulness..."

As he walked away—and I'm not kidding or exaggerating—my high was gone in an instant! I went from high to stone-cold sober. I actually felt a momentary urge to pull out a Bible and look up Lamentations. It was a strange, very real, sensation. But it passed.

It wasn't too long before my drug use began venturing beyond pot. I'd graduated to abusing prescription drugs and experimenting with meth and opiated hashish.

Ironically, at the same time, I was also growing in stature in the eyes of the officers and staff. I was doing well and thought highly of at my job. I was staying out of trouble in population, and many of my fellow inmates respected me. I had them all fooled. I was living a dual life. Behind the clean, responsible, polite front I put on, the reputation I was building, I was a real mess. I knew it.

Maybe a year or so later, and even more of a mess, I wound up a neighbor of Warner's—on Honor Block. See what I mean about how I was pulling the wool over everyone's eyes?

Warner's cell was clean. He kept it pretty bare, except for the rag rug on the floor, a small television on a desk, and an open Bible on his bed. That's all I ever saw walking by his cell. He didn't drink coffee. He didn't smoke cigarettes. He did have an insatiable appetite for sour cream potato chips. And I suppose if you're going to have a prison vice, that's a good one.

Hymns and verses of Scripture poured out of the man. Just about every conversation in which you'd hear his voice, a lyric, line, quote, or paraphrase would inevitably surface.

I had descended even deeper into drug use and folly—living on Honor Block, mind you—when I had another encounter with Warner. This one would stick.

At this point, I was full-on into the drug scene. I had a lot of connections—the bad kind. We'd managed to get a hold of a block of some opiated hash. One afternoon I had a group of guys join me, and we hung a privacy curtain across the front of my cell. We were sparking up the hash—tin foil and a toilet paper roll our paraphernalia—and fanning smoke out through the little window.

When we'd had our fun, and it had had its results, the guys left. I was absolutely wasted. I got up and was attempting to pull down the makeshift curtain and dissipate any remaining smoke and smell. I looked up to see Warner was standing across the way from my cell, arms folded across his chest. He was glaring at me. Our eyes met.

Once again, no exaggeration, in an instant my high was gone. Snapped sober! Same as before, Warner stood looking at me for what felt like a very long time. But this time he didn't say a word. After an uncomfortable moment or two, he shook his head, turned, and walked away.

It was sort of an epiphany for me. *What are you doing, Gene?* Tears filled my eyes. *Was this it? Drugs? Lies? For the "remainder of my natural life," was this who I would be? Was this living? I was in my mid-20s. What would this look like at 40? At 50? 60?*

"Morning by morning, new mercies I see..."

Warner's voice rang out early the next day, and every day. "Time to get up, everybody! God loves you!"

Somebody would shout, "Come on, Warner! Knock it off!" He'd laugh and go right on singing, bouncing with joy in his cell.

"Wake up, convicts! This is the day the Lord has made! Get up and sing with me!"

The cell block's chorus answered, "Shut up, Warner! It's too damn early for that sh..!"

But I wondered—*Was it too late?*

I found myself thinking about bigger matters than I ever had before. Out walking the track or the perimeter of the yard, I'd ponder things like *What is the point of life?* or *Why are we here on this planet?*

I may have even said "There's got to be something more" out loud. Even the God question crossed my mind: *Is God real?*

What did I really know of God? As I wracked my brain over it all, the strangest recollections surfaced for me—way back, from the Bible Stacy had given me some five years earlier, passages she'd highlighted came to mind:

> *Love is patient, love is kind. It does not envy, it does not boast, it is not proud. It does not dishonor others, it is not self-seeking, it is not easily angered, it keeps no record of wrongs. Love does not delight in evil but rejoices with the truth. It always protects, always trusts, always hopes, always perseveres. Love never fails.*

It didn't really mean anything to me except that I thought it was beautiful— I'd never experienced love like that. It sure did sound good.

Then there was:

> *I will show wonders in the heavens above and signs on the earth below, blood and fire and billows of smoke. The sun will be turned to darkness and the moon to blood before the coming of the great and glorious day of the Lord. And everyone who calls on the name of the Lord will be saved.*

I *certainly* didn't know what that meant or why it had stuck with me— but the imagery was cool. It sounded powerful, extraordinary, other-worldly.

I had no clue what to make of these strange poetic recollections coming to mind now. I had memorized some Bible passages without ever really having thought about it or intending to.

If you'd have asked me then, I had really formed an image of God in my mind like He existed, but in an out-there, disconnected, and faraway sense.

Those little snow globe toys we had as kids—the glass bubble with a scene inside and you'd shake it and snow would fly? I sort of imagined this world—and me inside it—as a little glass amusement for God. Every now and then He'd pick it up and give it a good snap ... and watch us all wallow down below.

While all this continued to happen in my head, I was assigned a new job delivering inner-office mail. My rounds wound all over the prison, and, best of all, took me back to the medical office where I had clerked a couple years earlier.

There I saw Joyce and Phyllis again. These two ladies had treated me like a peer, not a prisoner, for as long as I'd known them. It was now the highlight of my day, dropping in on them. The atmosphere in their office was so peaceful and warm, a real break from the chaos of the prison grind. And it was as if I'd never left—they were so personable with me, really caring.

It was around this point in time I'd also signed up for AA. I hadn't gone yet, but I had put my name on the list. One day I worked up the courage to share with Joyce and Phyllis what was happening in my heart—I'd determined to make some changes in my life, for the better.

"I've signed up for a self-help program," I told them. "I've been abusing drugs, getting high, pretty much the whole time I've been in here."

They were shocked. They had no idea. I hid it well.

"Gene, I'm proud of you for admitting you have a problem and deciding to get help," Phyllis said. "We'll support you any way we can." I knew she meant it.

"Have you heard about the Prison Invasion this weekend?" Joyce asked. "It's a three-day church event, happening all over the country. Gene, I really believe getting involved in a church would be a blessing and a support for you. You know that Harold and I have been a part of a great church for years. We love it."

I had heard about Prison Invasion '86. A group of local churches were coming in to host a big Jesus rally. I wasn't interested. It was true, Christianity was starting to appeal to me—my mom's faith, Harold and Joyce, Phyllis, and Warner, of course—I sort of wanted what they had. But I imagined it might be a better fit for me *later*, maybe when I got out of prison, had my life together.

Those few shining examples aside, most of the guys who called themselves Christians in prison turned me off. There were the ones who'd spout off all spiritual-sounding in one breath, and cuss like a sailor in the next. One guy in particular—they said he'd memorized huge sections of the Bible—and every other word out of his mouth was F-this and F-that. I wondered what version of the Bible he was reading...

Others would get in line for church services and meetings every time, but were the same guys hustling drugs or porn the moment the services ended. And then there were the SOs—sexual offenders. Church was popular with the perverts. It was all hypocrisy in my eyes.

Perhaps I wanted the genuine, but I was rejecting the phony. For me, Christianity would have to wait until I was at a place in life where I could be all in. It wasn't here. It wasn't now. Still, I didn't want to disappoint Joyce and Phyllis.

"You know, Gene, you can always sign up and still decide not to go," one of them commented.

That was my out! I told them I'd register and give Prison Invasion a try. But even as I walked out of their office, I was hard at work on a list of excuses.

The hypocrites came to mind—and besides, the church-going crowd wasn't the kind of guys I hung out with. It wasn't the jocks, the weight-lifters. It was the weaklings, the weirdos. I just couldn't imagine myself ... there.

A turbulent battle broke out in my mind. One minute I talked myself out of it. The next I was thinking about Joyce and Phyllis, and my mom. Back to the wimps—those guys lining up for church programs all look so frail and vulnerable. And then to Warner—nothing frail or vulnerable about him. 6'2", 260 pounds, a runner who blew up when he hit the weights. Warner wasn't a wimp or a weakling. And I'd never seen so much as a hint of hypocrisy in him. He respected everyone. He was respected *by* everyone. He was like liquid love.

Back and forth, the battle waged: *Maybe? ... No way! ... Well, it couldn't hurt ... Am I out of my mind?*

Before I knew it, it was Friday night—the start of Prison Invasion '86. *What was I to do?*

"It's easy," my brother Mike told me. "You just get out next to traffic, Gene, and stick out your thumb. Someone will give you a lift." It was really the only way to get around in my teen years. My girlfriend lived about 15 miles away. I'd jog several miles, but to ride part of the way sure made a difference.

I remember one of my first times thumbing a ride, a creepy old lady stopped. I climbed in. She had an old house frock-looking outfit on, smelled bad of moth balls, and appeared to have the start of a mustache growing. She kept taking her eyes off the road, looking at me, attempting to make small talk. She made me nervous. I kept my hand on the door handle the whole ride, ready to jump in an instant.

Another time, in a snowstorm, a police cruiser stopped.

"What are you doing out in this weather? Where are you going?" the cop asked. "Get in, I'll give you a lift."

I bragged to my friends about that ride: "I caught a lift in the back of a police car."

You never knew who would stop. Thumbing a ride was always an adventure, but it got you to your destination.

———————

Guys were filing by, lining up to go to the chapel for the first night of Prison Invasion. I stood at the door of my cell—watching. *Stick out a thumb, Gene.*

CHAPTER 7

REAL MEN
MAKE
COMMITMENTS

I had so many reasons not to go, an abundance of them, really. But in that moment, as so many guys were walking past, none of the excuses seemed good enough for me to remain behind. The next thing I knew I was walking in step with them. I was part of the crowd making its way toward Prison Invasion '86.

The chapel was on the opposite side of the prison complex—a newer-looking brick building, complete with tall stained-glass windows, a steeple, and a bell. Built by inmates, it had a vaulted ceiling, was outfitted with marble floors and surfaces, railings, an altar, and about 20 wooden pews on each side—I'd guess it could seat maybe 300 people.

I'd been there a few times over the years, for the Catholic service, stealing away a gulp of wine. It was designed to be an all-faiths sort of chapel: the altar could rotate and change to accommodate Catholic, Protestant, and even Jewish temple services.

As we approached, I was surprised to hear loud music pouring out of the place, and even more surprised to see dozens of men—volunteers from the local community—lining both sides of the path to the chapel entrance, like a gauntlet. They were there emphatically welcoming us. They all wore warm smiles on their faces, reached out to shake our hands, patted us on the back, thanked us for coming. You could tell, they genuinely cared that we had come to the meeting. It was an overwhelming experience. *Who were all these guys? Why did they care?*

Whatever nervous tension I'd felt about coming quickly disappeared.

I was glad I came. The music was so energizing, I forgot for the moment that I'd walked into church. I looked around, eager to take it all in. There were maybe 100 volunteers from the community and perhaps as many as 200 inmates, all crammed into that chapel.

I found my way about half-way up and took a seat on one of the pews. I watched as guys gathered, here and there, hugging, smiling, and laughing as they talked. You could tell who the volunteers were and who the prisoners were by the way they were dressed—but that was it. Guys were treating each other as equals, long-lost friends even. It was as if judgment had been checked at the door. It was unlike any other experience I'd ever had in prison. Hugs. High-fives. Laughter. I just sat there soaking it up.

And the music! I've mentioned it a couple of times now, but it really was a powerful part of my experience that night. I couldn't place it—nowhere in my church past had I encountered anything like it—drums, guitars, keyboards, singers. I had never been to any rock concerts, but I imagined they would have been like this. It was loud—not hurt-your-ears loud, but gets-your-foot-tapping loud. It was heart-lifting music. It felt good.

After a time, the music settled down and so did all the conversation. One of the visitors grabbed a microphone and asked everyone to find a seat. He began by thanking the prison and administration for allowing the volunteers to come in, as well as the chaplains for their support. Then he thanked all "the brothers"—the Christian prisoners who were there—who came to worship God and His Son, Jesus Christ, who he introduced as "King of Kings and Lord of Lords!" At that, the place erupted in cheers, whistles, and applause.

Guys shouted, "Hallelujah!" It startled me. Never before had I imagined shouts, whoops, and cheers in church.

The speaker then explained that the men who were there volunteering were from the local community—men from diverse backgrounds and different churches.

He said, "These men love God ... and they love you!" It rocked me. The smiles and hugs offered by strangers—I was serving a life sentence without the chance for parole ... I'd been using drugs—that they'd be excited to see *me*, that they'd love *me*—it was unbelievable. *What did I have to offer? What was in it for them?*

Music started again. It was engaging. I was paying attention to the words. I'd never listened to gospel music before. I liked it. Between every couple of songs, somebody quoted a verse from the Bible. They all seemed to hit me like the verses highlighted in the Bible Stacy gave me—poetic, thought-provoking, intriguing.

One by one, a few guys were invited up to share what God had done in their lives. It felt like each one of them was speaking directly to me.

The first one said he was a drug addict until Jesus changed his life. He thanked God that his desire to get high just went away when he trusted Jesus, and he didn't even experience any withdrawals. Just like that, he had a clean start.

Another man talked about how he'd been involved in dealing drugs for years. He had done some pretty violent stuff, even took shots at people. "Everything changed," he said, "when I met Jesus."

Still another shared that he'd been in prison for a few years when God miraculously opened the door for him to have a second chance. Those words "opened the door" absolutely penetrated my world.

With each story, the "church" erupted in applause and cheers. And my heart pondered ... *Could it be?*

After their sharing, an older gentleman was invited up—the featured speaker. He took the microphone out of its stand. He stepped away from the lectern. It was obvious he was speaking from his heart, not from notes. He talked about Jesus—that Jesus was sacrificed on the cross to pay the cost of our sins. And not only ours, but the sins of the entire world. Once again, I felt as if this man—whoever he was—had come to speak directly to me. I was nervous. *Did everybody feel like this? Why did I feel this way?*

I contemplated his words. *If Jesus died for everyone's sins—did He die for mine? That's what that means, right?*

After his message, the music team played a few more songs. The speaker then gave an invitation: "If you'd like to make a commitment to Jesus Christ as Savior and Lord, come forward."

I promise you, I never sat so still as I did in that moment. I thought if I moved so much as a muscle, he would look my way and think I was responding to his invitation. I might have even held my breath. *I wasn't ready for this.* The idea appealed to me, but not now. *Not tonight. Not any time in the near future. Someday ... maybe.*

A bunch of guys went forward. Then the preacher invited believers who were backslidden, or who had stumbled in their faith and wanted to re-dedicate themselves, who wanted a fresh start, to get out of their seats and come forward. Another handful of guys went down. I sort of had a good feeling for all those guys—like "good for you" as they walked. It just wasn't my thing.

When the service was over, I headed back to my cell. The preacher's challenge—"make a commitment"—and the stories those men told turned over and over in my head. I may have admitted to myself that I wanted what those men had, really wanted it, but I worried. *Commitment?* An honest appraisal of my life to that point revealed I quit things when they got tough. Relationships. Jobs. Goals. *Why should I expect a religious commitment to be any different?*

But that night I felt strangely different. Things in my life suddenly didn't seem as hopeless or discouraging as they had just a few hours earlier. The music, the sharing—they had an abiding effect on me. I was surprisingly upbeat.

Then the strangest thing happened. A friend walked by my cell. I called out, "Hey! How you doing?"

"Good," he answered.

And, without so much as a thought, "Hallelujah!" came out of my mouth. He stopped in his tracks, looked back at me—I think he thought I was nuts. Maybe I was! *Did I really just say that?*

I slept well that night. I woke up a couple times, turned over, and dozed back off to thoughts of the service, the music, everything. The next morning, I felt great. I sprang into my routine.

After breakfast, I met up with some friends to work out. It had been my Saturday morning pattern for years. Exercise really did wonders for my self-esteem and was a great stress-reliever. The bigger and stronger I got, the more respect I felt from my peers. It also helped me play tackle football for 11 years straight, and to dominate guys who were even bigger than I was.

During this Saturday morning workout, I noticed the group of Christian volunteers from the night before was given access to the prison yard and housing units. They walked around in small groups, engaging inmates and inviting them out to the services that evening. You know how it goes—sort of like when a used-car salesman is making his way toward you across the lot. I was wishing them away. Of course, one of the men approached me.

He tried to strike up a conversation about my workout, how long I'd been training, and how often. I was polite but short in answering. He quickly turned the conversation.

"Did you attend the service last night?"

I told him I had been there.

"What did you think?" he asked.

"It was good," was all I offered in reply.

"I hope you'll come out tonight," he said. He looked as if he intended to stay for a while, interrupting my workout. I did my best to avoid it, focusing on the task at hand. After a few minutes, he bid me farewell and moved on to talk with some other guys.

I felt a little guilty, like maybe I should have allowed for the interruption—maybe I should have been more receptive.

About an hour later, as I was wrapping up, another volunteer approached me and introduced himself as Bill. Bill was a square-jawed man with thick, black hair and tanned and wrinkled skin. He looked to be in his late 50s.

He shook my hand with a big, disarming smile, "Man, I am so glad to be in here sharing the Gospel with you brothers!"

Again, the notion that he thought of us as brothers, and acted as if he'd known us for a long time, made a distinct impression on me. I'm not sure whether I thought it was good or bad—just very, very different.

Without so much as a pause, he launched into sharing his story with me. "You know, I was an alcoholic for 10 years before I met Jesus," he said. It grabbed my attention, of course—it hit close to home. Everything he shared seemed to reflect my family, my experience growing up. "Man, I came home every night, staggered into the house. If not for Jesus, I'd probably be dead."

My father came to mind. He was diagnosed with cirrhosis when I was only 20 years old and died just a few months later. Bill was telling me Jesus helped him stop, probably saved his life. He had my attention.

"You know, Gene, it was my mom who kept after me. She always invited me to come to church with her. So one day I did," he said.

"Yeah? What happened?" I asked. *Had I really just invited the conversation to continue?*

"The music was playing..." Again, his words struck a chord in me. The music had grabbed *my* attention ... "And the preacher gave an invitation for anyone who wanted to come forward and accept Jesus as Lord and Savior. I went forward ... and got saved."

That phrase—"got saved"—several of the guys had said it the night before. It seemed very transactional to me: get up, go forward, get saved. I wondered what it really meant, what took place inside when you made that commitment. *What did it feel like to get saved?*

Bill continued, "I tell you, the desire to drink was gone. For me, it was a brand-new lease on life."

Mom came to mind. My whole childhood, even when there was no money, Mom somehow strung enough pocket change together to buy cheap beer. I hated it. It controlled her. The stumbling, bumbling—slurred speech, repeating herself over and over—living in deep poverty, yet she always had a drink.

She had used those same words, "got saved." And it was miraculous. I'd seen it myself. Her visits—everything had changed.

Bill reiterated the invite, saying, "I hope you'll come to the meeting tonight. I'll save you a seat."

As he excused himself to go talk to some other guys, I just kept thinking about how his desire to drink was immediately gone. Then I appreciated his offer to save me a seat, but I wish he hadn't offered. Now I felt obligated to show up.

I invited my friend Harry to come with me on Saturday. I knew he would be skeptical—he'd keep me grounded in reality.

Walking into the chapel on Saturday was just like the night before—many volunteers lined the way to the entrance, shaking hands and warmly greeting everyone. There was music playing again, but this time a little more subdued—guitars and voices only as opposed to the full band Friday. I led Harry to a seat, pretty much the same place I sat the night before. Inside I was experiencing a strange tension—I was at once both excited to be there and very nervous. I couldn't wait to see what was going to happen. I also couldn't wait to get out of there. How strange is that?

Some of the guys who were with me started joking and teasing. Henry nodded toward a man in front of us with his hands raised in praise. "Hey, Gene, that guy is missing a few fingers!" Wouldn't you know, I turned and counted: eight, nine, 10. He had all his fingers. I looked back at Henry. He was laughing so hard his whole face was red. I couldn't help but laugh, too. I immediately felt guilty. I didn't want to be disrespectful of the service, of the people who were genuinely partaking. I tried to position myself from that point on to not get caught up with the pranksters.

When the music ended, the preacher got up and spoke about Jesus' death, burial, and resurrection. He spoke of Jesus, again, as God's Son. "Jesus gave His life for us on a cross so we don't have to." I wasn't sure what to make of that. I remembered my childhood years in the Catholic church—Jesus hung up there on a cross. But I'd never equated that to me, to my need, or to His hanging in my place. The preacher was connecting Jesus' death to my life in a way I hadn't heard, hadn't considered, before.

Just as they had the night before, the service ended with an invitation. Just as I had the night before, I sat very still. Glued to my seat. *Not me. Not now.*

When the service was over, they announced we'd have some extra time before officers would escort us back to the housing units—time to meet and greet. I knew what that meant: guys coming up to me and asking if I'd made a commitment that night, asking me if I was born-again.

I wanted to disappear. I imagined the conversation. They'd ask, I'd say "no" and mumble through some lame excuse, because I really didn't have one. I tried to avoid making eye contact with anyone, certain it would be seen as an invite to "Come talk to me." I wanted to portray, instead, "Just leave me alone."

Just as I anticipated, I heard the conversations starting all around me: "Hey, did you make a decision tonight?" and "Are you born-again?"

I thought, *Get me out of here!*

"Hey! My name is Larry," he began. This guy stood about my height, a full head of silvery hair, wearing a bright yellow boating jacket—Members Only or Dockers, I'd guessed. "Did you make a commitment tonight?"

"No," I replied.

"Has anyone counseled with you this weekend?"

Again, "No."

He smiled at me like he knew me ... like he cared.

I'd seen Larry the night before. He was up in the balcony playing the keyboard. He told me he was a local pastor, and that he and several men from his congregation were there as counselors for the event. Larry had been to Camp Hill many times before, visiting with different inmates. This was the first time I'd met him. I wanted nothing to do with this conversation, but I didn't want to be dismissive like I had been to the guys in the yard earlier.

"How long have you been a Christian?" I asked him.

"Since I was four years old," he replied. *Was he putting me on?*

"You have been a Christian since you were 4?"

"Yeah," he said, "and I knew God's plan for my life since I was 5—to be a missionary."

Immediately my thoughts turned. *What's wrong with me? If a four-year-old can sort out this Jesus stuff, why couldn't I? If a five-year-old can know his life's direction, what the heck was I doing at 26, without a clue? Zero. Nothing.*

Here I was living this dual life—Honor Block, drug hustler, hypocrite, filled with guilt and shame.

As our time ran out, he handed me his card. "Pastor Larry Titus, Christ Community Church, Camp Hill" it read, with an address and phone number.

"Listen, Gene," he said, "If there is anything you need—a Bible, some clothes, books to read, anything at all—you write or give me a call." He meant it. I could tell.

On the way back to the cell, I realized—I really enjoyed the conversation with Larry. I was glad it happened, glad I met him. Imagine if my tactic of avoiding eye contact had worked, if I'd have been left alone as I wanted. This felt ... like someone cared.

"Did you talk to those church folks?" Harry asked. "Man, they're gonna get me a new TV! Maybe some sneakers! I just played along! That was awesome, man! We gotta go back tomorrow! You hear me, Gene? I'm gonna get a new TV!"

Harry saw it as a chance to score. I wasn't sure what to make of it myself, but I knew it was genuine. In light of Harry's response, I felt convicted for having Larry's card in my pocket. I reassured myself, *I had no intention of using this caring man just to get stuff.*

I didn't sleep well that night. I tossed and turned, thinking back through the service—the music, the message, my conversation with Larry afterward. I returned over and over to Larry's saying he became a Christian at 4 and knew

God's plan for his life at 5. *A child gets this, but I can't?* I was so frustrated. At one point, I sat up on the edge of my bunk—I couldn't believe it ... I wished I had made a commitment.

They'd had a church service every Sunday morning during the nine years I'd been there, but never had I even considered going. Here I was, this Sunday, up and on my way to church. It wasn't as exciting as it had been the previous two nights. This felt a little more like a church service than a rally. I slipped in and sat in the very last pew. Harry was with me, mumbling something about getting some new shoes.

I had a bit of a strange sensation. *What if those guys had been put in my path—the guys who shared on Friday night, Bill and his story of being delivered from alcohol on Saturday morning, Larry on Saturday night with his story of being a Christian since he was a child—what if it wasn't coincidence, but providence, that all our paths crossed?*

I don't remember who the preacher was that Sunday morning. He'd been brought in from out of town by Prison Invasion. He held my attention, though. I heard and considered every word he said. It even seemed at times like he was looking right at me as he spoke, which is saying something, since I was sitting in the back row of a packed room.

The preacher kept saying, "Real men make commitments." The notion stabbed at my conscience. It bothered me—I was certainly good at a few things, but I'd never made and followed through on a commitment other than my GED. I had no greater purpose in life.

"You don't give Jesus a try like you try out a brand of peanut butter. Jesus is the Son of God," he emphasized. "You need to be a man, and make a commitment to follow Him."

Once again, a message just for me. I needed to make a commitment to Jesus.

Then came the invitation. I was sweating. I gripped the pew I sat on with both hands so tightly my fingers turned white. My stomach clenched, tighter and tighter. I willed my feet into the floor as if they'd grown roots. I was holding on for dear life.

All around me, men were standing and going forward. "Just slip out of your seat and come," the invitation was repeated. "We'll wait."

I was feeling really awkward, like they were waiting just for me.

Just then, Bill, the man who had shared his conversion story with me on Saturday morning, approached. "You can do this, Gene," he said. "Jesus wants you to accept Him."

I wanted to say yes, but I couldn't form the word. I was speechless.

Two more guys joined Bill. "We'll go with you," one of them said.

You can't even begin to understand—and I struggle to express—the tension of that moment.

My world was spinning. I wanted to go. Badly. But my legs weren't moving. I was frozen. I was terrified. I felt like a coward. It was, and is, completely inexplicable. I couldn't tell Bill what was happening. It was as if I couldn't make up my mind—one brief second it was *I'll go* and the next was *Don't you dare!*

Suddenly, it just happened. I leaned forward. I was on my feet. I dropped my winter coat on the pew behind me and started to walk. I was very aware of each step, putting one foot in front of the other. I didn't stop until I was at the altar. I must have moved pretty quickly, because I looked around to see Bill and the other men scrambling to catch up, to stand at my side.

"Let's kneel down and pray like Christians," Bill said.

We knelt down on the hard marble floor. It's like everything else around us fell away. In that moment I wasn't aware of anything beyond our little prayer circle with God. Bill led me in a sinner's prayer. I remember saying, "Jesus, I believe you died and rose again for me. Please forgive all my sins. I want to be saved." And we ended it, "Jesus, come into my heart today. Amen."

It sounds cliché, but the moment I said those words, I felt as if a ton of weight rolled right off my back. I felt as if chains fell away and I was free.

How ironic is that? I, a man in prison for life without the possibility of parole, and very much secured around the clock, felt utterly and completely free. Well, I did. I absolutely knew something had happened within me, but I wasn't at all sure what it was. I was just thankful.

Bill gave me a hug. And when Bill hugged you, you knew you'd been hugged! Other guys patted me on the back, shook my hand—they were all rejoicing over me. Bill asked if I had a Bible several times during our conversation. I told him I did, the one Stacy had sent me. He said I should start reading it as soon as I got back to my cell.

When I walked out of the church and headed back to my cell, I was excited. That word "Hallelujah!" came back to my mind. I had no idea what it meant, but I wanted to say it, to shout it out. I yelled it to a couple of guys along the way—they looked at me like I was crazy. I smiled. I laughed.

I opened the Bible the moment I got back to my cell. I thumbed through all the highlighted passages—some in the Old Testament, some in the New Testament. I looked back at some I had enjoyed before—Acts 2 and 1 Corinthians 13 among them. For the first time in my life, I realized Jesus was real and not just some fictional character you hear about in church. He was so very different from the impression I'd carried all those years.

Maybe an hour had passed when some friends, the guys I normally worked out with on Sunday mornings, stopped by. "You coming to work out?" they asked.

"I'm going to pass today, stay here, and read my Bible."

They were shocked.

As they left, I continued reading. At some point I looked up and noticed the centerfold pictures I had hanging on the wall of my cell. They'd been there for years, part of my surroundings. Suddenly I was aware of them in a different way—I wanted to take them down. I tore them into small pieces and flushed them down the toilet.

Beyond the pictures, I opened a curtain that kept my cell dark. I wanted light—I couldn't get the place bright enough. I had a sudden urge to clean my cell. I neatened everything up. No explanation. It just felt like the thing to do. Then I went back to reading. I devoured the gospels. And I got on my knees and prayed several times, for people, over situations I knew I couldn't handle without God. I experienced a divine connection.

While I prayed, an old friend of mine, Danny, came to mind. I said, "God, please forgive me for hurting Danny."

My first impression of God speaking to me came clearly to my conscience: "I'm not Danny. Go ask him to forgive you."

The thought of going to him was paralyzing. Ever since that time I tried to apologize to my mom for staying out all night and drinking with my friends, and it went so disastrously, I couldn't imagine a positive outcome.

As I walked to his cell I imagined how this might go. He might reject me. He might laugh at me. I started to hope he wouldn't be in his cell. But he was—sitting on his bunk watching a Steelers football game.

Our eyes met, and it felt like my tongue was stuck to the roof of my mouth. I had to concentrate to even form the words: "Danny, you got a minute?"

He looked confused. It had been more than a year since we'd spoken. "I want to apologize for mistreating you. I was a jerk. You didn't do anything wrong. Please forgive me." *Man, was that hard!*

Danny stood up, walked to me, and gave me a hug. "It's all good," he said.

My apology was received. I was relieved. I walked back to my cell feeling freer than I had in years. God was at work, breaking the ties that bind, setting me free!

I wrote several letters. I wrote to everyone I could think of, really. I wanted people to know about the decision I'd made to follow Jesus. Family members. Friends back home. Several of the girls I'd met, Stacy for sure. Kathy McGuire, the pastor's wife in Michigan who mistakenly received my letter back in 1978—I suddenly became aware of so many junctures along my path where God had shown up. I wanted them all to know.

That evening I made a phone call, too, to my mom and step-dad. Mom was overjoyed. I could feel her emotion through the phone. Whatever else would happen, now we had eternity in common.

My step-dad, Loren, said, "That a boy! I'm so happy for you." It felt so good to connect with both of my folks on this new level.

Somewhere around midnight I began to rub my eyes. They were bloodshot, weary. I was falling asleep sitting up. I prayed one last prayer, "Lord, I want to know you and your will for my life." I laid down, closed my eyes, and fell fast asleep.

CHAPTER 8

THIS IS THE DAY THE LORD HAS MADE

Warner was the first guy I told I got saved. He put his hand on my shoulder, looked me straight in the eye, and said, "When you get up every morning and sweep the dust out your cell, Gene, sweep the sin out your life by confessing it. And never lose the love of God. You will always be effective as a Christian. You confess, 'This is the day the Lord has made, and I will rejoice and be glad in it!' You understand what I'm saying?"

Tears poured down my cheeks.

The next day was Monday. Prison Invasion '86 was history. I was back into my routine. But something was different. Very different. I woke up and followed Warner's advice. I picked up my cell, and then went to putting my heart in order. I prayed and committed myself, "This was the day the Lord had made, and I will rejoice in it!" And it felt great.

I noticed a difference right away—I was calm. At peace.

Everything in prison life is frustrating. Little things like moving from one place to another, taking so much time, having to wait for them to buzz a gate, buzz a door. Usually those little inconveniences drove me nuts. I'd get agitated, aggravated, short-tempered.

But here I was, present in the moment, and ... fine. Content. Even happy. If I had a moment I was forced to stand still and wait on something or someone, I'd say, "Thank you, Lord!"

For the first time in my life, I became really conscious and aware of those around me. I'd look over at the officer I was waiting on and ask, "How are you, today?" And it wasn't an empty question. I cared. *Who was this new man? What had happened to the old Gene McGuire? I don't know! But I liked the change!*

My inner-office mail rounds took me back to Joyce and Phyllis midmorning. I couldn't wait to tell the ladies what happened. But when I came through the door, things felt a little odd to me—a little tension filled in the air. I didn't know at the time but found out later that they had spoken to another inmate who attended Prison Invasion over the weekend. He told them he hadn't see me at the meetings. Both ladies were under the impression I hadn't gone and were disappointed for me.

"I went to the services," I said.

Their mood changed in a heartbeat. "You did? What happened? Tell us!" They both beamed with hope.

I tried to form the words "I got saved," but as I did, I just broke down crying. I don't mean a teardrop. I mean *sobs*! They helped me sit down. They closed the office door. I cried like a baby.

"We thought you hadn't gone," Joyce explained. "Jeff was there. He said he didn't see you."

I tried to explain—"Hundreds of guys ... I sat still the first night ... the next day ... then Sunday I went forward..." The more I spoke, the more I cried. And it felt so good. I was telling my story.

I sat in the office with them for probably an hour. Joyce gave me a Bible she had in her desk. Of course, I already had one back in my cell. But this was a meaningful gift. I accepted it, thanked her, and would cherish it. She also told me about her pastor, suggesting I add him to my visitor list so he could come visit with me. I agreed I would.

That afternoon and evening, I wrote several more letters. I wrote Pastor Larry a long note—probably 10 pages long—telling him everything that had happened on Sunday and thanking him for having shared with me Saturday. I believed it was his words—about his belief in Jesus at 4 and knowing his life's calling at 5—that God used to reach my heart. Even more than the preacher on Sunday, it was Larry's genuineness and kindness that had touched me. I wanted him to know that. I wanted to thank him.

I must have been a sight. I was crying, kneeling, praying, reading my Bible. Guys kept looking in as they passed by, asking, "Gene? What's up?"

I'd tell them I got saved, and tears welled up in my eyes. Some of them thought I went crazy. A few guys came by to test this new commitment of mine out for its merit—a couple Muslims, a Jehovah's Witness. They were checking my newfound theology.

"You know Jesus isn't God, right?" the JW, named Smokey, asked.

I didn't know what the heck he was talking about. I didn't care. "Here's what I do know," I told him. "I believe in Jesus ... and I got saved!"

Smokey had no sooner walked out my door before I shot over to Warner. "Is Jesus God?"

"Yeah, man. Let me show you." He showed me some verses. I was a sponge, taking in all I could absorb.

"It's practical, Gene, this new faith of yours," Warner emphasized. "Put it to practice."

I must have given him a puzzled look. He told me a story. "Man, when I was a new believer, I didn't quite get how it worked. I was sitting in my cell praying about a job. 'Oh Lord, I need a good job in here! Help me, Lord!' This old dude came by and asked, 'What you doing in there?' I said, 'Praying for a job.' Next day that old man came by and saw me praying again. He said,

'The Lord knows you need a job—you prayed about it yesterday—now go put yourself in the work line so He can give you one.'"

Warner's ministry in my life cannot be overstated, even though his manner of ministering was very understated. He didn't preach. He related. I can't count how many times he posted up outside my bars, just telling me stories. He was always there when I had a question. And he always had an encouraging word. I even got to a place where I loved his singing! God used that man in my life—I'm so thankful for his friendship and the example of faith he provided us all.

Tuesday night was Bible study night. I wanted to go. But I was nervous. All the guys get in a long line—everybody sees you. I stepped out into line, and realized I had this bright red Chaplain Ray Bible in my hand. Chaplain Ray was a radio preacher who had a huge ministry among inmates around the world. I don't know where I got this Bible, but there I was. I had this momentary panic—*Oh my gosh! It's bright red! Hide this thing!* I was tucking it under my arm. I laugh, looking back.

I started to look up and down the line of guys. My eyes met a man ... my heart skipped a beat ... I'd met him before.

It was many months earlier, before I'd been saved. It was during that time, I'm sure, the Lord was really pursuing me. I was angry, wondering what the point of life—of all this—was. Back when I was trying to figure it all out, finding any and every reason to refuse Christianity. Sitting out in the yard with a bunch of guys, someone pointed to this one old man, saying, "That dude is a child molester!"

I don't know what I was thinking. But in response to that comment, I jumped to my feet, walked straight up to him and grabbed his arm, "Hey, pervert! How many kids have you raped?" I shook the man and walked away. I heard guys laughing.

And ... I immediately felt terrible for having done it. *What the heck was that?*

This night, our eyes met a few times during the Bible study. Near the end, the Chaplain asked, "Anyone want to share anything?"

I raised my hand. "I just got saved," I said. "And I owe some of you guys an apology. I picked on some of you. Said some stupid things. I'm sorry." My eyes filled with tears. I felt so ashamed. Guys said things like, "It's all good, man." They clapped. Someone patted me on the back.

Before we lined up to leave, I walked over to the older gentleman. "Do you remember me?" I asked. He nodded. He absolutely remembered me. "I'm really sorry..."

He nodded again, saying, "I accept your apology." I gave him a hug.

With every new experience in Jesus I felt little burdens lifting, weight I'd been carrying, taken off my soul. At night when I hit the pillow, I couldn't wait until the next day, to see what new mercies awaited me. It was a race to wake up!

Very soon after I sent my letter to Pastor Larry, I got one back. He was thrilled that his testimony of being saved and knowing the plan for his life at such a young age touched me—and that it was definitely a God thing. He told me he'd gone home that night and the enemy went to work on him. He worried, thinking, "That was a stupid thing to say to a guy serving a life sentence." But God knew better! He asked me to put him on my visitor list so he could come see me. I did.

By the time Pastor Larry came to visit, I'd already had some visits from Joyce's pastor, Pastor Mike, a Baptist minister from town. I don't know how else to describe it other than to say the visits with the two of them couldn't have felt more different.

Don't get me wrong: Pastor Mike was a very nice guy, and I'm thankful for the time he invested. His visits felt formal, almost as if he carefully kept things at arm's length. He never told me much about his personal walk with the Lord. And there was a lot of pressure—to be a follower of Jesus I needed to do this, do that, work on this, work on that.

Pastor Larry's visits, by contrast, were very casual—like family. He told stories, shared about his own faith-struggles. He was transparent. And he had a great sense of humor—we laughed and laughed together.

The one thing about every visit with Pastor Larry is that while he didn't give me assignments—you need to do this or that—every time he left I wanted to go back and pray, and read the Word, search out whatever little lesson of truth he'd mentioned. Time with him made me desire to grow closer to God—there was no mistaking that.

Pastor Larry came once a week. We'd eat lunch out of the machines in the visiting area, talk, study, pray. His manner of mentoring and discipling me was so natural, so simple. Some days I'd go out there whining to him, "This guy did this" or "That guy did that."

And he'd just look at me and say, "You gotta love 'em, Gene."

"Yeah, but..." I'd start.

And he'd say, "No *buts*, Gene. Love 'em."

It was right around that time that I got my first glimpse into one of the not-so-attractive realities of church—divisiveness. The Bible makes it clear: there's one Lord, one faith, one baptism. But we don't always embrace and embody that truth very well.

Joyce's pastor began to express concerns to me about my friendship with Pastor Larry. "He's a Charismatic," he said. "He doesn't believe what we do."

I struggled to understand. It seemed like jealousy to me. I mentioned it to Larry—and he had nothing negative to say about Pastor Mike. The contrast was stark. On one hand, Pastor Mike seemed to be delivering up an ultimatum, either/or ... while Pastor Larry was happy for any and all Christian ministry ties I'd established. It became a real source of discomfort in my visits with Pastor Mike.

After a little, while I told him I wanted to focus on discipling under Pastor Larry. While I had appreciated his time, I didn't want to visit with him anymore.

This is one of those things about Christians that must grieve the heart of our God. He's our Father. We're His children. And yet we've mastered the art of dividing up, in an "us against them" mentality, over any number of things. It was a difficult experience. It wouldn't be my last.

Remember the guy I worked around who always used profanity? Well, Clyde was his name. Everyone said he'd memorized huge passages of the Bible, but every other word out of his mouth was profane. Now I'm a new believer, getting to know the others who profess faith in Christ, and who do I run into? Clyde!

God used Clyde to speak into my life. I learned two all-important lessons from him. First, he taught me a simple method to commit portions of the Bible to memory. He had indeed memorized a lot. I was impressed. I asked him how he did it.

"The key is five," he said. "Read it five times; say it out loud five times; then say it without looking five times. Then you got it."

I'm not sure the formula or the number "5" was really key—perhaps for others it would be 10 ... or 20. But the fact that this guy had committed so much of God's Word to memory using a repetitive pattern meant I knew I could do it too.

The second lesson I learned from him was a little darker. I realized that it is entirely possible to read God's Word, even memorize it, and still not have it touch your heart.

And I knew I didn't want that to be my path! I wanted to read the Word, memorize the Word ... and embody the Word.

I can't begin to describe the joy that came when I began spending quality time with Jesus. I started each day at His feet. Reading His Word was my heart's desire. It brought many other lessons.

One day I came across 1 Peter 1:15: *But just as he who called you is holy, so be holy in all you do; for it is written, "Be holy, because I am holy."*

The idea of holiness seemed so distant to me. I'm an inmate, serving a life sentence, surrounded by other inmates—not exactly the best context in which to ponder holiness! So I decided I was going to be holy, like a resolution— me, holy, starting now.

I struggled. I beat myself up with every slip and failure. I became so frustrated. No matter how hard I tried, how often I prayed, how long I fasted, how much Scripture I memorized—I couldn't be perfect.

I met the prison's Catholic priest one day. I told him of my salvation, and we talked for a while about things we had in common—our belief in Jesus as Lord and Savior. I told him I really wanted to accomplish something big for God, and that I was wrestling with holiness. It was like a reality slap when he said, "Gene, God isn't interested in your performance. He's interested in you—a relationship with you."

He encouraged me to spend time reading the New Testament. I soon realized holiness isn't about performance but about submission. In Hebrews 10, I read: *"Sacrifices and offerings, burnt offerings and sin offerings, you did not desire, nor were you pleased with them"*—though they were offered in accordance with the law. Then [Christ] said, "Here I am, I have come to do your will."

It takes the submission of our will to do the will of God. Only through submission—not performance—will I experience holiness. This realization was *liberating* for me! It can be for you, too. God doesn't need you—He wants you!

Next on my list to confront was the manner in which I'd been leaning on girls, those who visited me, for my validation. I wanted God, and God alone, to be the source of my worth.

I remembered back to Stacy, who told me that I had to find my happiness and fulfillment in Christ, not in her. I was really upset at the time I read that in her letter. But here I was today, realizing she had spoken truth to me all those years ago.

I apologized to the girls who were writing and those coming to see me. I told them all of my new relationship with Jesus Christ—and while I hoped we could still be friends, that was all I envisioned for us from that point forward. A couple of the girls were touched by my honesty. Our friendships really blossomed. They went on with their lives, and over the years they married and brought their husbands to meet me. God is good!

Visits with Mom after we were both believers took on added meaning as well. It was a joy to hear about her involvements in her church, and to have her ask about my faith, my studies, and my ministry involvements. I ventured into some more difficult areas, seeking healing and renewal. I asked her questions about my dad. She had a tendency to get defensive. I really didn't want her to—I simply wanted to know more. Who was my dad? Beyond the memories of his drunkenness, showing up at my games and embarrassing me, the fact that he was a Yankees fan and was absent for most of my life's most important moments ... who was he? It was hard for her to talk about. I realized their marriage was a very painful part of her life.

We talked about that night, too. She wanted to cover for me. "It wasn't your fault, Gene," she'd say.

"I made choices, Mom," I'd reply.

"It was Bobby," she'd argue.

But I didn't want to shift blame. I wanted her to know that I owned it.

Flashback. I was 14. It was an Austin Healy. It looked so cool. Taking it for a spin—high adventure for sure.

"Let's do it," Mike said. "No one is home. We'll get it back before anyone is any the wiser."

"Okay," I agreed.

We snuck over to the neighbor's driveway, started it up, and we were off. It was so awesome. We wound around the town roads, up and over hills, leaning into the turns, the wind blowing our hair. We lost track of time. Our quick joyride ran long.

"Sh..! We better get back before we're found out," Mike shouted.

We raced for home. At the very moment Mike pulled into one end of our neighbor's half-moon driveway, we saw them pull in the other side. In the panic, Mike scraped the car against a four-point plow next to the garage. We bailed out and ran.

Later, when everyone asked us what happened, we tried to shift the blame: "We saw some black guys from the St. Michael's School for Boys hanging around..."

It was a lie. And everybody knew it.

Our joyride cost us a summer's worth of work on the neighbor's farm to pay off the damages. Thinking back, I felt guilty for having lied, for having tried to shift the blame. We were guilty. I was guilty.

———————————◦———————————

I realized: Mom harbored guilt. In her mind, she was the one who said "go ahead" that night when Bobby suggested taking me along. For years, was carrying that burden. The "If only..."

Now it was my turn to minister to her. "Mom, it wasn't you. It was me. And what the enemy intended for harm, Mom, God has made much—and will make much more of still—in our lives." In Jesus, we had a fresh start.

Therefore, if anyone is in Christ, the new creation has come: The old has gone, the new is here!

I was experiencing the truth of 2 Corinthians 5:17. He was bringing the lesson home to my heart.

From the very start of my new faith, one thing that has never failed to overwhelm me is how gracious and loving God is when we approach Him. So different from how we often respond to one another, out of impatience, inconvenience, or offense, God welcomes us when we come before Him.

Every approach we make is cushioned by His mercy and grace. Because God is love, He keeps no record of wrongs, no ledger of past offenses to hold over our heads. Like the father in the prodigal son parable in the Bible, He stands waiting with open arms, not a boney finger of judgment to point out our wrongs. His forgiveness is freeing, welcoming. He says, "Come!"

In much the same way, our forgiveness of others is freeing. It frees us from bitterness and hurt. But that is such a tough lesson to learn and apply. In my newfound faith, as I prayed and studied, as I went to Danny and others I'd hurt, apologizing and requesting their forgiveness, another list of people came to my mind. They were individuals who, over the years, had hurt me—

people I needed to forgive.

———————◦◦◦———————

I don't remember exactly what I said, but I do remember the sudden crack and intense sting on the side of my head. I remember the collective gasp of my seventh grade class at the realization that our math teacher had hit me. And I remember looking up just in time to see him twisting his huge class ring around on his finger—the ring he'd very intentionally whacked me with. I grabbed the side of my head; a welt was rising, quickly the size of a golf ball. Pain coursed through me and curse words spewed out of me. I ran out of the classroom, dazed and hurt, both my head and my pride.

I blew right out the door, across the field and off school grounds. I hitch-hiked home. The school called my mom to report my absence from afternoon classes. I explained to her what happened. She told me to report to the principal's office first thing in the morning. I did. I told him everything just like it happened—I cracked a joke, other students laughed, and then the teacher hit me. The principal called for my math teacher, who walked in and denied the whole thing. "It never happened," he said. "I didn't hit you."

Are you kidding me? There was still a knot on my head!

The principal concluded, "You need to be punished."

He was talking to me!

"We can either suspend you for three days or administer corporal punishment with a paddle. Which will it be?" *Me? I need to be punished?* Talk about adding insult to injury.

I chose the paddling. Three whacks with a paddle, each seemed to satisfy the math teacher all the more. And honestly, I developed a hatred for my math teacher in that moment. It might sound silly, but I couldn't let go. For years to come, whenever recollection of this singular moment in my adolescent life surfaced, hatred and bitterness burned. I often daydreamed of vengeance, of getting him back, of him finally getting his due.

———————— ❊ ————————

My dad—I had to forgive him. He drank his way right out of our family. He drank himself right out of my life—out of his own life—dying when I was only 20. He'd deprived me of having a dad. I prayed that God would help me let it go, help me forgive him. I did.

My mom—I had to forgive her. Those years when she didn't live up to her role as a mom deprived me of a healthy mother-and-son relationship. I had to let it go. I prayed for the grace to forgive, to move on in my relationship with her. I did. We did.

Others—guys who had done me wrong, stolen from me, lied to me, offended me—I had to forgive them. As often as things came to my mind, I prayed for God's grace, to let go, to forgive, to begin new and fresh.

Then there was that recurring pain, shame, embarrassment ... an abiding bitterness and hurt—my teacher. It was like a deep bruise, the best way I can describe it. Every now and again that bruise would get poked, the pain awakened.

Then one day, I'm certain it was God Himself who poked the hurt with Matthew 18, and the parable of the unforgiving servant. I really felt the Lord prompt my heart and say, "I've forgiven you, and yet you won't let this hurt go!"

I tried to argue. "Lord, I have forgiven him." Then I felt the Lord direct me to another passage. And there it was, in black and white—Matthew 5:43-45: *"You have heard that it was said, 'Love your neighbor and hate your enemy.' But I tell you, love your enemies, and pray for those who persecute you, that you may be children of your Father in heaven."*

The Lord spoke to my heart: "You say you've forgiven him, but you haven't blessed him!"

And the second part of that passage stirred my heart. I want to be my Father's son. I broke down, praying for, and, yes, asking God to bless, my teacher. No more desire for vengeance.

When I set him free, I was also set free—I wanted God to bless him. And you know what? A huge burden, that had been slung around my neck for more than a decade, fell away. Gone!

And then there was Bobby.

"Get over here, man. Give me a hand," Bobby was sliding furniture and rolling up throw rugs.

"What are you doing?" I asked.

"Let's clean your mom's house for her. Let's scrub the floors!"

It was just a couple days before the murder. He'd arrived in town, was staying down at the lake with my brother, and he bounced in to do some chores to help my mom. This was the Bobby I knew. He always looked out for her. She mattered to him. And I was so naïve.

I had no idea he was on the run from the law at that very moment. I had no idea he was conspiring—had spoken with my step-brother Sid trying to find a place to rob—to pull together some cash.

Sid wasn't the sharpest kid. Bobby had used him, really. I had no idea that his wife and children weren't on their way as he told us, that they were wondering where he was and what he was up to. He was living a dual life—a deadly one—and he had me totally snowed.

Why had he wanted me to come along that night? Was I a part of this plan? A slip-up? Was he using me? If and when I allowed myself to go there—Yes, I had made choices that night, but if I had stayed home and gone to bed...

I had crossed paths with Bobby briefly, early in my time at Camp Hill. I was working in the infirmary when they turned it into a psyche ward. Bobby had earned himself a stay in psyche lock-up—stabbed his counselor or something like that. When I saw him, he was breathing murderous threats toward Sid—"I'm gonna kill that motherf..."—and insisting he had to get out of Camp Hill. "There's too many young guys here. I'll kill someone if I stay."

And he tried. He attempted to stab a staffer in the neck with a ballpoint pen. They shipped him out. I was grateful no one died ... and that he was gone.

Beyond that, I only ever heard of him through my mom or sister. "He stays in touch with Arlene," I'd hear. "Tells her of all the fights he's getting into."

"He got into some trouble at Frackville," they'd say. "Added another few years onto his sentence." This was the real Bobby.

I wrote to him after I got saved. He sent a note back. It began, "I sit here in my cell and wonder how I wound up here, with two life sentences plus 75 years..." He went on to chronicle his time in prison and his violent escapades—he stabbed someone, had taken hostages, I don't know what all. This was Bobby's reality.

I'd have to forgive him. And, like with my teacher from long ago, I'd have to forgive and bless him. The difference was, *I wanted to.* For all that had happened, Bobby was my cousin. I loved him.

Mess of a life we've both had—I *still* love him.

CHAPTER 9

PLAYING BY THE RULES

I had been working out all afternoon in the yard. I was covered with sweat, a layer of dirt caked onto me that had kicked up around the iron pile. I had one thing on my mind—a hot shower. The Lieutenant blew his whistle. More than a thousand guys from Unit 6 headed in from the yard. You can imagine how it goes. Some guys are always in a hurry, pushing through the crowd. Other guys drag their feet, blocking progress. It was inevitable: guys bump into each other, brush off one another, as we were herded in.

This day, an inmate shoved past me and ran his hand quickly up and down the back of the guy's shirt directly in front of me. Just as quickly, he stepped to his right and vanished in the crowd. The guy he'd touched spun around and stared at me, as if I had done it. He grabbed at his shirt, realizing something was wrong.

When he turned forward again, I noticed his t-shirt had four or five long slices, running from his shoulders down to his waist. Blood began to soak through.

He stepped out of the crowd and stumbled toward an officer. By the time he reached help, he collapsed to his knees. The officer lifted his shirt to reveal what had happened—his back had been carved up, like shredded meat. "That's what snitches get!" guys shouted as they passed. "Snitches get cut up!"

I don't know when it was instilled in me. I'd heard it from my earliest days—we all did: "No one likes a tattle-tale." In prison, it's a matter of survival. This incident was another reminder.

Images of that man's sliced and bloodied back didn't leave me for a while. I could picture the razor blade in the aggressor's hand, imagine the pain, see the damage. I wondered how deep the wounds were, how many stitches it took to close them. But I didn't wonder why it happened—it didn't matter. You see nothing. Hear nothing. Say nothing. You mind your own business in prison.

I was satisfied that the early conflict I'd had—Nookie blowing me kisses—had left me with a pretty solid reputation. There could be hell to pay if you gathered the reputation as a snitch.

Prison culture polices itself, for the most part. Conflict is rarer than you might think. Many times, if something happens, you only hear about it a few days later. That said, there's nothing to prevent a fight, or a stabbing, or even a rape, if it's planned out. If something boiled enough, it could explode.

Horse was a large man—as the name suggests—who kept to himself. One of the Sergeants, a guy named Dell, was always after him, dogging and harassing him every chance he got. Horse took it, seemingly refusing to be provoked. Then a day came, and he went flat out murderous.

Horse was mopping the floor. The Sarge walked by, said something. The next thing you knew, Horse was beating the officer with the mop, the metal mop-ringer, the bucket—everything from which he could fashion a weapon. He beat the man to a pulp. Help came, but it took time, and then it took even longer to get Horse off the fallen officer.

Stuff like that has heavy consequences. Horse was segregated for more than a year. You can bet he had significant time added to his sentence. But that's how things happened. Simmer ... boil ... BOOM!

Most of the time it happened spontaneously. Guys would get frustrated and vent. A violent outburst. Maybe words, threats, a punch, a shank in someone's side—and it's over, just that quick.

Or it could be a defense mechanism. You've heard the term *fight or flight*? Well, there's not a whole lot of room for *flight* when you're incarcerated. You'll be found sooner or later. So *fight* becomes instinct if you're backed into a corner. Usually—if you handle yourself well—it's a one-time test, and then guys leave you alone.

The metal-grated catwalk above my cell made noise when inmates walked on it. You got used to the sound and cadence of normal steps, normal traffic up there. It became background noise. You'd notice right away if footfalls were heavier. Stomping around up there was a good indication a fight broke out. You'd look up and see shadows moving; something was going on. Then a crowd would gather, everyone jockeying for position to see.

Those footfalls escalated one day, and I looked up to see Lil' Sam, with his head down, swing a wooden floor brush at Scott. Scott side-stepped the swipe and drove down on the top of Sam's head several times with a toothbrush. I bet it lasted all of about 15 seconds. Sam backed up, and Scott walked back inside his cell.

I'd known both men for several years as we lived on the same range. What had happened was clear. Scott was a known homosexual. Sam thought Scott might like his company, and made an advance. Guess again! Sam quickly realized he was no match for Scott and retreated.

He came downstairs and walked toward me. His face was soaked—I thought at first it was sweat. As he got closer, I noticed it was blood running down his face, dripping off his nose and chin. I handed him a towel. He put it to his head and in an instant it was blood-soaked.

"How bad is it, man?" he asked.

I took a closer look. Sections of his skull were loose and moving beneath his scalp. "Man, you have to get to medical!" I told him. "It's bad!"

He turned, reluctantly, and walked up the range, my once-white towel pressed to his head.

An hour or so later, I was called to the Security Office.

"What do you know about Sam's injuries?" I was asked. "What happened? Who did that to him?"

The officers held up a clear plastic evidence bag with a very bloody towel inside—AK4192 clearly stamped on the corner of it.

You know the rules. "I saw Sam walking toward me ... bleeding," I replied. "You'll have to ask him what happened."

It was a big manila envelope addressed to me from the Pennsylvania Board of Pardons. It was my opportunity to apply for commutation of my sentence—a lifer's only hope of release.

I'd been anticipating this chance for a while. I had served 11 years at this point, gotten my GED, become a believer in Christ, and was building a support team around myself, both those who wrote recommendations for me and those who would support me if I were released.

Essentially, the commutation process is a plea for mercy to the Governor, through the Board of Pardons. It's not a means to argue legalities, it's rather a Hail Mary attempt to convince the system you are worthy of a second chance despite your life sentence. It allows you an opportunity to, in your own words, explain why you think your sentence without the possibility of parole should be commuted to a life sentence *with* the possibility of parole. There are five members on the Board: it's chaired by the Lieutenant Governor and includes the Attorney General, a crime victim representative, a corrections expert, and a psychiatrist.

The form is a questionnaire:

State briefly the details of the crime for which you are
requesting commutation.
Why do you believe your plea for mercy should be granted?
Specifically, why do you need commutation?
How have you conducted yourself while incarcerated?
How have you contributed to the community, and what
efforts have you made to rehabilitate and improve yourself?
Will you have employment, and where will you reside,
if released?

The first nine years of my incarceration I hadn't done much in the way
of personal achievement beyond earning my GED and taking a year's worth
of college courses. I'd played organized tackle football and softball. But the
reality was, I spent much of those early years watching television, passing
time. In subsequent years, I'd been involved with the Pennsylvania Lifer's
Association and helped raise money for some charities. But with this first
commutation filing, I felt underprepared. It was a reach, and I knew it.

Nevertheless, I had to start someplace. I took a few weeks to answer the
questions as thoughtfully as I could. I asked a few other guys who'd been
through the process for advice. They were happy to help. I wrote and rewrote
answers—wore through a bunch of erasers and filled a few wastebaskets in
the process.

I never really arrived at saying what I wanted to say. Everybody I knew
who had filed had been denied. There were guys with 20-plus years and a
stellar resume who were getting turned down. They warned me, "Be prepared
for your first several requests to be denied." They spoke of it like a process—
get in it for the long haul.

I felt like there were a few real positives to my initial application. First, I
hadn't committed the murder. Second, I had become a Christian and had a
very solid support network around me, inside and outside the prison. Third,
I had no opposition from the victim's family or the District Attorney's office.

Prior to filing my petition, I wrote to both the sentencing judge and the prosecutor. I asked for their opinions on my application. I was discouraged with the response of the judge—he wrote back saying he had no opinion on the matter. The District Attorney, on the other hand, supplied me with a supportive letter, and put the burden on me to prove I was prepared to be released.

I asked friends and family to supply letters of recommendation. I wound up with a dozen or so—and they meant the world to me. To know I was loved and cared for, that there were people who believed in me and would stand with me ... I can't even explain how special that is.

I packaged it all up, prayed over it, sent it off, and asked all my friends and family to join me in praying for God's favor ... and certainly for the Board of Pardons' and the Governor's favor.

As I awaited word, I spent a lot of time in prayer. I remember waking up around 2AM to pray, raising my hands in the air and praying for God to open doors. I came away from that season of prayer confident that I was His son and had adopted the attitude of a servant. Whether or not a Board of Pardons weighed in favorably, I knew I had received God my Father's approval.

I definitely wasn't the same person who'd come into prison 11 years earlier as a 17-year-old high school sophomore. I had accepted full responsibility for the choices I made and for my behavior. I was deeply remorseful. I honored those in authority over me and was embracing, to the best of my ability, the servant nature of my Lord.

It didn't take long. Less than two months after filing my petition, I received a two-line response from the Secretary of the Board of Pardons: "The above named applicant's petition for Commutation of a Life Sentence did not receive the two votes needed to be granted a public hearing. Therefore, his request is denied."

They'd told me to expect a denial my first time out. But I'd be lying if I said I wasn't disappointed. I was rejected, and I wanted to know why—they don't tell you. My counselors told me to keep trying, but, in the meantime, to put a few more years into my sentence. What helped me the most was to focus on that servant attitude. *Servants have no rights, and so what right did I have? Why was I upset?*

I got on my knees and thanked God for the opportunity to have filed, and to have prayed so fervently to Him for my release. I spent the next couple of days calling and writing letters to notify Pastor Larry and my family and friends of the Board's decision.

Pastor Larry sent me a note quoting Romans: *All things are working together for the good to those who love God and are called according to his purpose.* He emphasized the word ALL. He also told me to add a couple from his church to my visiting list. They were attorneys willing to help with my next petition.

I received an unexpected invite in June of 1989. A prison counselor asked if I'd be willing to sit down and talk with Pennsylvania Senators John Heinz and Arlen Specter about prison overcrowding. Recommended by the superintendent, I'd be one of three inmates. It was a very serious matter for us—I welcomed the opportunity if it would help relieve the situation.

We walked into the visiting room. Lights and cameras surrounded a table in the middle of the room with a couple of microphones on it.

The senators sat behind the table wearing dark suits and ties. As they rose to shake our hands, shutter clicks and flashes went off. They welcomed us to take seats beside them. I sat down next to Senator Specter.

I don't recall exactly what everyone said. We dialogued about overcrowding at Camp Hill, the conditions we were experiencing and the effect it was having on the inmate population. What I remember clearly is that, as soon as I'd finished my remarks, Senator Spector turned and looked directly into the cameras and said, "This is why we need more money to build more prisons!"

Really? I thought. *That's the answer? Build more prisons?* It felt like we'd been used. Like we were nothing more than a political photo-op. *Hey taxpayers, pony up! You don't want these guys walking your streets!*

Just as quickly as they'd greeted us, we were dismissed. If the politicians didn't get enough press for their cause that day, they certainly would just a few months later—in October, they'd hit the mother-lode.

CHAPTER 10

THE INMATES TOOK THE ASYLUM

"They're rioting!" somebody shouted.

Guys rushed over to the window to see what was happening. We saw an aggressive crowd of 30 or more inmates, moving from one area of the compound to another—like a school of angry fish. As they moved, Corrections Officers lie in their wake, beaten and bloodied.

It was October 1989. I was working as a para-teacher with the Residential Building Apprenticeship Program at Camp Hill. Our shop was located on a corner of the Education Building. Twelve inmates at a time participated in the program. I was the first lifer permitted to participate in some two-and-a-half years.

George, our teacher, was a good-hearted Christian man. He wasn't a CO. He was a tradesman-instructor, employed by the education department to teach everything from cabinetry to residential building skills. The men who took his classes respected him. He had a passion to help train and prepare inmates for re-entry into society. You knew it was important to him—he often shared stories of guys who'd been through his program and who were, now, succeeding on the outside.

Each day in the shop began the same way. George spent the first 30 minutes with the guys sitting around a table, teaching specific skills and handing out assignments. He might begin by explaining, in detail, something like placing a sill plate or corner bead trim. But he would inevitably include something personal of his own life experience. It was real.

So was whatever was happening outside the window that day. I could tell by the look on George's face. As he was getting word of what was happening on the phone, he turned white as a ghost.

There were some 2,600 men at Camp Hill—an institution built in the 1940s to accommodate about 1,400 juvenile offenders. Overcrowding? Quite an understatement.

Men who had left, but violated their parole, were brought back to complete their entire sentences. At the same time, the State of Pennsylvania determined the best way to curb the recidivism was to keep inmates incarcerated longer, so parole was more often denied.

Double-celling—doubling two men up in a space intended for one—had begun six or seven years earlier. They'd added eight modular housing units. They, too, were packed beyond capacity.

It wasn't just the living space that was in short supply. Programs couldn't accommodate the swelling numbers. Many of the guys were without jobs and healthy activities. It meant hours and hours of idle time. Which is asking for trouble. And when paired with a case of severe understaffing—it was a recipe for disaster. A perfect storm.

There was a new Superintendent named Freeman. Visually, the guy reminded me of pictures I'd seen in school of Adolf Hitler—not the little mustache, but everything else. And he wasn't friendly. He was harsh. He'd taken away incentives. He'd changed rules about visitation that impacted the annual family picnic—a real favorite of the inmates. Food quality fell way off as a part of cost-cutting measures. Have you ever had scrambled eggs that were green? I'm not exaggerating.

Stress and anxiety amped up with every change, and no one in authority bothered to dialogue or explain. Inmate complaints fell on deaf administration ears. Morale deteriorated. Frustration mounted. Anger brewed. You could tell that the slightest spark would set off an explosion.

Alarms went off. My heart began to race.

"Beat their asses!" one of the guys at the window shouted.

This wasn't good. George was on the emergency line, face frozen, eyes wide, mouth open. "Get away from the window," he ordered. Nobody moved.

The swarm of inmates moved out of our sight to the left. A group of officers came running in pursuit. They spun on their heels right in front of us, running in retreat now as the angry mob reappeared, pursuing them. A couple officers who were older or overweight were quickly overcome by the crowd and knocked to the ground, violently kicked and stomped.

"Come away from the window! I'd like everyone to come and sit down in the classroom area," George ordered again. "The prison is on lockdown— we're staying right here."

This time guys listened. We sat down together. Waiting. George looked nervous. He had to be wondering what was happening, and if he was in imminent danger.

About 10 minutes later, an inmate worker stood up to peer out the window again. "Here comes a group of officers—in riot gear," he reported.

Again, men rushed to the window to see. This time George didn't order us back. He didn't say a word. The first thing I saw was a dozen or so wounded officers and tradesman, laying all over the grassy sidewalk area. Then I noticed maybe 25 officers, with helmets, shields, and clubs, advancing in formation toward a crowd of inmates. They beat their clubs on their shields, hoping to intimidate them. It didn't work.

Things turned in an instant. The officers—in full riot gear—broke rank and ran for their lives, the mob of inmates, now likely more than a hundred strong, chasing. It was a shocking sight to see. Just as before, the older officers were overtaken, beaten to the ground. Each time the crowd moved on, victims were left behind; men with bloodied faces, hats ripped off their heads, and, curiously, the back pockets torn off their pants.

One of the inmates looking out the window pointed to the pockets and said, "Got their wallets."

Chaos reigned. In the distance, I saw an overweight tradesman trying to get away. It played out in front of us like a pathetic game—predators stalking prey. They appeared to toy with him, taunting him. He'd grabbed a fire extinguisher in an attempt to ward them off. Surrounded, he turned on the inmates with its spray. It only took a moment for them to knock him down, seize the tank, and hit him over the head with it. He lay bleeding as they left him.

George hung up the phone. His voice trembled, "They're setting fires—the other side of this building is aflame. We're to wait right here."

Several things crossed my mind. Obviously—*FIRE!* And, *we're staying put?* Then the realization—*There's a lot of highly flammable stuff in a wood shop! Of course, there's also a lot of sharp tools.* I wondered just how long it would be before someone in the angry crowd outside, or someone told to wait inside a burning building, figured that out. I could tell by looking at him that George was thinking the very same thing.

They had taken hostages and set fires on the other side of the building we were in. The room next to us was the commissary. It went up like a tinderbox. Our room began to fill with smoke.

"Everyone, sit on the floor," George directed.

Just then security officers ran in and asked, "Everything all right?"

I could only think in sarcasm—*You mean aside from the fact that there's a riot out there and ... a FIRE IN HERE?!*

George told them all of the inmates in his program were present and accounted for—and safe for the moment. With that, they told us to stay put a little longer. *How much longer?*

The smoke thickened. My heart raced. I was scared. Several frightening scenarios flashed through my thoughts. *What if rioters broke into the Education Building and took teachers hostage?* Most of us, I thought, would defend George, but there were a few guys who might not. *What if the fire broke into where we were, or blocked our way out?* I don't know how long it had been, but we couldn't see the ceiling above us anymore—and the cloud was descending. *What if they forgot about us?* We were trapped, and they weren't opening any doors.

Officers finally returned. *Our rescue?* You'd think so, but no. They ordered us to stay still "just a few more minutes" as they opened a rear door and began escorting staff members who had been assaulted in other areas of the building through our shop, to medical help. Most looked exhausted, like they'd been running. Some were bruised and bloodied. A few had torn clothing. One thing was obvious—they all wore terror on their faces. Once the victims had been evacuated, we got up assuming we were next. No. The officers closed us in again. *Were they serious?*

George said, "They'll be back for us."

I don't know how much longer it was. Too long. When he realized we were out of time and no one was coming, George directed, "Let's get out of here!"

We couldn't stand. We had to crawl out on our bellies. We made our way down a hallway to the far end of the building where we met two officers in riot gear. They escorted us to a far recreational yard, a secured area, safe from the chaos. From there, looking back, we had a clear vantage: smoke, very black and very thick, rose high above the Education Building—right where we had been.

As the sun set, those of us in the recreation yard walked the perimeter, watching, talking, in disbelief. We followed every new development— another fire truck arriving, officers moving to new positions. Somewhere amid all the commotion it occurred to me that it was night—and I was outside. I hadn't seen the night sky over my head in more than 12 years, since the night I was incarcerated. I took in the starry sky. *Beautiful!*

Around midnight, an officer appeared in the yard and said they had the institution back under control. We'd return to our housing units soon. *Was it over?*

As they took us back to our cells, under escort, we walked past the badly burned backside of the Education Building. There were piles of things stacked and still burning—the remains of desks and chairs that had been dragged out. There was a golf cart flipped over and torched. Trash littered the grounds. No clean-up had begun. Everywhere you looked, things were broken, defaced, disheveled. It looked like a war zone.

Walking into my unit, Honor Block, I noticed the officer's desk was sitting low to the floor. "They ripped the legs off and used them as weapons, like clubs," one officer said to me when he saw me notice.

At long last, I was back in my cell. Even so, I couldn't relax.

One of the guys across the range asked, "Did you hear what happened to Officer Johns?"

My heart sank. Johns was one of the nicest COs on the Honor Unit.

"He opened a secured door and they bull-rushed him." He went on to describe how one inmate with a hammer struck Johns in the face several times "'til he quit moving!" The tower officer fired shots at the ground near them to chase inmates away. "He's alive. Barely," he concluded.

I couldn't imagine it. Not that any officer deserved to be beaten, but

Johns was one of the really good guys—a caring guy, with a wife and family. This whole thing made me sick to my stomach.

I wondered how many officers and staff members had been hurt, if anyone had been killed. I prayed it wasn't as bad as it looked. I prayed for Officer Johns.

Power was off to some cells—mine included. I asked a friend in a cell above who had power to drop an extension cord down. I was able to power my TV and turn on the news. The reporters shared a statement the Department of Corrections' Public Relations office had given them—there had been an uprising, the institution was now on lockdown, all inmates were secured in their cells, an investigation was underway. It was quite an understatement of what had actually occurred.

There was a lot of buzz traveling around the unit—the rioting inmates had negotiated to release their hostages for the chance to meet with the administration and discuss the overcrowding. That meeting was scheduled for lunchtime the next day. "Now we're getting somewhere," they said. I couldn't imagine what, if any, concessions would be made.

This protest and these negotiations would likely fare no better than the protest sit-in inmates had hastily organized just a few weeks earlier.

It was a sunny September afternoon. Guys started boasting, "We're not gonna take this anymore!"

Word circulated, "When they try to call us in from the yard this afternoon, we're not coming in! Everybody just sit down, right where you are, and refuse to move. We're gonna force them to hear us, force them to listen."

It was something to do. In prison, guys are always looking for something to do. So inmates rallied around the idea. When the call went out for prisoners to come in from the yard, we all sat down. Hundreds of guys—no one moving. Officers scratched their heads. Half an hour passed. Our protest was working!

Until additional COs spilled into the yard. Someone in charge shouted, "Okay, start taking 'em to the Hole!" They grabbed up a couple of guys and dragged them away. They came back, grabbed a few more, dragged them off. Then a couple more. Inmates were looking around at each other. What next? I was thinking, *Well, this has been a lot of fun, but I don't want to go to the Hole!*

Apparently, everybody else was thinking it, too.

First a couple guys hopped to their feet and walked quickly toward their housing unit. Then a few more. Guys around me fell in line ... and I joined them. You've never seen such an orderly procession inside! Just like that, protest over.

The concessions administration made that day? They graciously offered a dozen or so protestors a week's worth of all-expense-paid enjoyment in Camp Hill's finest isolated accommodations.

About a week later, there was—what they called a "riot" at the time—a small protest in the dining hall. Guys erupted, shouting, tipping over tables, throwing trays. A few sustained minor injuries. Administration's concessions that time? They put us *all* on lockdown for a couple days.

Prison admin negotiating with unruly inmates? Don't hold your breath.

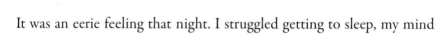

It was an eerie feeling that night. I struggled getting to sleep, my mind raced back and forth with violent images of chaos. And a Scripture verse brought peace: *For the grace of God that brings salvation has appeared to all men, teaching us to say no to ungodliness...*

This was different than the sit-in and the food fight. Inmates had gotten the attention of authorities. But admin wouldn't bargain. No way! To do so would only encourage this sort of violent uprising in the future. They had to put this rebellion down. This was going to go south. The only question: *How far? What would tomorrow bring?*

The next morning, officers handed brown bags with hard-boiled eggs, white bread, and a carton of milk to every inmate for breakfast. That was our reward for the kitchen having been damaged. There was a lot of chatter, even boasts, about all the changes administration would make. Folly. I knew it.

The noontime meeting happened. It was short. It didn't take long for inmates to walk out, angry. Word spread quickly, "Administration doesn't care!"

"Were staying locked down for a long time!" one inmate shouted. Things were being said—who knows what was truth and what was exaggeration, but it all heated emotions. Boiled the rage. The place was a powder keg.

It was around 7 that evening that a huge commotion stirred—inmates began shouting, chanting, and rattling the bars of their cells. Someone yelled, "They're out!"

I looked out a window and saw silhouettes of guys running by. I grabbed my little plastic mirror and held it outside my bars to see down the range. The officers up front opened the big metal doors and ran, abandoning their posts. The doors stood wide open, and it was only a matter of seconds before a group of inmates, in masks and hoods, came running in. They brandished club-like weapons in their hands and raced down the unit, shouting, "We got f...ing hostages!" and "We've taken over the whole f...ing institution!"

Pop! The door to my cell was suddenly triggered to open. Several doors on the range opened. I panicked. Inmates had gotten hold of the controls and were opening cells. *This wasn't good!* I wanted no part of it. I slid my door shut, figuring I'd stay out of the way. *Pop!* It opened again! I peeked my head out and looked down the range to see if I could find my friends—wondering if their doors had opened, too.

I looked outside and saw inmates running around wearing the officers' riot gear, beating clubs on shields. "Now who runs the institution?" they yelled. "We're gonna f... them up!"

My friend Andy, who lived in a completely different building came running up, disheveled, out of breath, sweating profusely, and wide-eyed with fear, "They got the whole place, Gene!"

Four other guys showed up right behind him. They were all asking, "What should we do?"

I said, "We're gonna pray!" I wasn't trying to be spiritual. I had never felt so out of control and surrounded by so much chaos in all my life. I pulled the guys into my cell. We got in a circle and started praying.

A couple guys walked down the unit with a clipboard. "We know who the snitches are," one of them shouted. "We're comin' to get the rats!"

I had no idea who they were looking for—I knew I wasn't a rat. But I also had no idea whose names were on their list. I was worried; someone could die if authorities didn't get this place back under control, and fast!

Not long after they passed, a guy named Albert dashed into my cell. "Gene! I'm on their list! I need to hide! Help me!" Albert wasn't a snitch, but he fit that stereotype—he got along with COs. He wouldn't have the chance to explain.

Before I knew what had happened, he dove underneath my bunk. He was there for hours. It was a sick feeling—a group of guys moving around with a hit list, and one of their targets is hiding under my bed...

After we'd prayed for a while longer, we decided to group up and walk down the cell block to see if any of our friends needed help and to check out what was happening. We picked up some desk legs along the way in case someone tried to attack us—we had no idea what to expect. Then we heard one of the leaders of the riot shouting instructions on a bullhorn: "Don't fight one another! Fight the power!" They made it clear: authority was the enemy.

When we walked outside I couldn't believe my eyes. The unit looked like a scene from the movie *Mad Max*. There were huge fires burning in the courtyard. Guys were yelling, banging on stuff. Someone ran by wearing a football helmet, wielding a chainsaw, acting like a mad man. Another guy rushed past pulling oxygen and acetylene tanks and a torch. Rioters had broken into the gym, the school, the furniture factory—anything they could fashion as a weapon they seized, anything that would burn they set on fire.

To give you an idea of the scope of this bedlam...

There were six housing units in the population area—three on one side, three on the other—each held about a few hundred men. Guys were marching out of one unit and straight into the next—they looked like army ants—gathering stuff to add to the fires. I stood there in the courtyard hoping to hear the Lord tell me what to do. I was scared. I knew enough to stay out of the way of those inmates on a mission to feed the flames. I watched someone throw a fire extinguisher into one huge bonfire in the middle of the yard. The explosion rocked the place. I felt the ground shake. Some poor clown must have been standing too close, his body vaulted through the air. He hit the ground, rolled over, and took a good look to be sure he still had all his limbs!

Guys tore down a segment of a barbed-wire fence and repositioned it to prevent anyone from entering—barricading themselves in the courtyard. Buildings that had been set on fire began to collapse. Helicopters flew overhead, their searchlights piercing the smoke, illuminating the chaos below.

The group of guys with me now numbered about 10. I realized I hadn't seen my friend Ernie. I told them I wanted to go down to his cell to see if

I could find him. As I approached it, two inmates stood outside the door wearing bandanas to cover their faces. I walked up to the door, paying them no mind, I saw him lying under some covers.

I said, "Ernie, are you okay?" He didn't respond.

"He's fine," one of the guys by the door told me. I took a closer look. It wasn't Ernie at all. It was one of the Corrections Officers they'd taken hostage. I returned to the guys I was with and told them what I'd seen.

We decided to head back over to my cell. We hung out there, snacking on some commissary items I had until they ran out. We tuned in to the news coverage—they showed the prison, choppers overhead, prisoners running about, and fires that reached high into the night sky. We talked about what was happening, how we thought it might end.

We feared the officers would retaliate and treat us as if everyone had taken part in the uprising. The reality was that while a couple hundred prisoners caused all the ruckus, doing all the damage, the majority of us—thousands of inmates—sat peacefully in our cells waiting for help to arrive. In other words, there were bad bad guys and good bad guys. We hoped the authorities would realize that. While we were all inmates, we all weren't their adversaries.

Outside my window I could see dozens of emergency vehicles gathered, their headlights all fixed on the prison. The reds and blues of their emergency lights bounced off every surface, and sirens echoed through the night. It sure looked to me like they were planning, perhaps even staging. Their response would come ... and soon.

We were all exhausted. Someone asked, "What time is it?" It was nearly 4:00 in the morning. We weren't the only ones tired. Apparently, rioting takes a lot out of you—the chaos outside began to quiet over the next few hours.

Somewhere around 7AM we were all stirred. A voice over the public address system announced the State Police would be coming in at 8AM sharp.

We inmates could choose to surrender to them—or prepare to be taken by force. A lot of us were ready to surrender. A handful of guys started for the gate only to have inmates with clubs and sticks block their way—"You ain't going nowhere!" they threatened.

A struggle broke out. Punches were thrown. More guys wanting to leave rallied, amassed a crowd, and literally barreled through the resistance. Those resisting moved aside, and the barricade was removed.

I could see outside the main gate a large group of officers had formed, many on horseback, all heavily armed, positioned maybe a hundred yards away. They were preparing to bring force. An officer began to shout on a bullhorn that all inmates should surrender, crawling out of on their bellies. I knew the officers wouldn't be able to tell the peaceful prisoners from rioters. I imagined that, even in surrendering, we had a beating with police batons coming. I put an extra sweatshirt and sweatpants on beneath my prison uniform to help cushion blows.

We got on our hands and knees and began our crawl. Officers shouted, "On your bellies! Lay flat!" I looked around—hundreds of inmates were crawling out.

Suddenly, a huge commotion broke out to our left. J-Block, referred to by the inmate population as "The Projects," housed some of the loudest and most intimidating guys in the prison. Only the biggest and toughest officers were assigned to that unit. J-Block inmates had flung their door open, while about 50 of them came storming out, hooting and hollering, shouting and chanting—ready for a rumble. We all knew they meant it—these dudes were crazy!

A bunch of State Police officers charged toward them. We heard the pump of a bunch of shotguns. You've never seen 50 men hit the ground faster! They were crawling like the rest of us.

We were all flexed-cuffed, hands behind our backs, and stood up and placed in groups of 10 to be escorted to a large recreational yard. They marched us over to one side and had us kneel down along a chain-link fence. Within an hour or so, there were probably more than a thousand of us corralled there. State Police on horses rode back and forth, closer and closer, forcing us back, telling us to get closer together. "Keep your heads down!" they shouted. "No looking around!"

A few of the officers seemed to enjoy intimidating guys. As one pressed the crowd back, an inmate who wasn't paying attention got knocked to the ground by the horse. Other officers rushed over and snatched the guy up, reprimanded him, and made him apologize to the horse … made him give the animal a kiss. *That sort of behavior wasn't going to help defuse this situation.*

But I had other things to worry about. My shoulders burned from the way my hands were cuffed. And I ached—as I'm sure all the guys did—bound like this and forced to kneel for so long. I struggled and shifted my weight, desperate to find some relief. Some of the guys' flex-cuffs were so tight they dug into their skin. Mine were actually a little loose. Once I figured that out, I worked my hands back-and-forth a bit and eventually slid them free. I quickly repositioned my hands in front of my body and slipped the cuff back on.

Officers kept a close eye on us. One asked why I was cuffed in front. I said, "Shoulder issues." He moved on.

They kept up the intimidating manner of riding their horses right up to us, backing us up, smashing us against the fence and into one another, every 30 minutes or so through the day.

By the middle of the afternoon, they realized we hadn't eaten yet anything, so they brought in some take-out containers with chicken and mashed potatoes and dropped one in front of every inmate. It was obvious—the way guys were bound, they'd have to bend over, face in the dish, and eat like dogs if they were to eat at all. I can't convey how degrading the experience was—these men treated like animals. With my hands in front I was able to feed myself, and I helped a few of the guys around me, feeding them with my fingers.

Another reality set in. It was unseasonably hot for late October. And the extra sweatsuit I put on for padding? I promise you, I was paying for that decision. The sun was cooking us. I was unbearably warm. I never prayed so hard for sundown!

I suppose one blessing in the midst of the wait was that, with my hands in front of me, I was able to pull out a small pocket-Bible and read. I read silently to myself at first, but then began to read out loud for the guys around me—they all wanted something to focus their minds on.

It was well after sunset when buses started pulling into the prison yard. Big Greyhound and Trailways passenger buses, bright yellow school buses, and transport vans of every possible size and variety streamed in like a parade.

I told my friend Dwayne, who, by this point, was in tears from the pain in his shoulders, "I bet we're getting on those buses. They're taking us all out of here." And of course, they started loading guys from the far end of the yard first. Our wait would continue much longer.

It was around 10PM when a Trailways bus pulled over in front of us. Guys, on their knees, inched their way forward, jockeying for position—we all wanted out of there. It didn't matter though. They were pulling guys out of the crowd. A State Policeman stood right over me and Dwayne. He looked at us, the long gold stripe down his pants leg seemed to run the distance between his eye to mine.

"You want to get on that bus?" he asked.

"Yes, sir," I replied. He pointed to the two of us, and other officers helped us to our feet—the first time we'd stood since morning.

I was in the front seat as the bus pulled out. It was a huge relief. I wanted out of there. For the first time, we got a look at the extent of the damage—

now I understood why they had to move us. There was little left. Housing units, support buildings, offices—destroyed. Building after building was smoldering, in ruins. I thought things looked bad that first night, but this. This was utter destruction. A war zone.

It was about a 90-minute ride to another state corrections facility, Smithfield. They unloaded us. The intimidation continued. The officers were clearly not amused at what that had occurred at Camp Hill. They herded us in, strip-searched everyone, and processed us into small holding cells for the night. At least it was a safe place to finally get some rest. But I laid there a long time replaying all the events I'd seen the last couple of days. I was in disbelief. *Had it really happened?*

I thought about George. I wondered if I'd ever see him again. I recalled one of my early encounters with him—a memory that brought a smile to my face. He told me and another inmate to go find the studs in the wall that divided our classroom and the hallway. We knew that wall studs were 18 inches on center, so we figured if we found one, then we'd be able to locate the others. I grabbed a claw-hammer—and the other inmate followed my lead. I started knocking holes in the drywall. Without yelling or scolding, George ran out of the office to stop me as I wound up for my third or fourth swing.

"Start at one end of the wall with a measuring tape," he said with a smile.

Those holes I'd punched—they remained in that wall the entire time I participated in the program.

I thought, too, of the overcrowding at Camp Hill. It really was out of hand. But even with those conditions, I witnessed God's favor over my life and the lives of others who trusted Him. A bunch of the Christian guys spent quality time in Bible study and prayer. We'd held public foot-washing services on the housing units and had communion together. I had a deep conviction that this is how the Body of Christ would grow, patterned for us in Acts 2. It was sure discouraging to think that those days, those relationships, and those experiences were behind us. I'd have to leave it all in God's hands.

At some point I drifted off to sleep. I awoke the next morning to an officer's voice: "Hey! What's your name, inmate?"

CHAPTER 11

THE TIMES AND PLACES OF YOUR HABITATION

They don't ask you where you want to go or how long you want to stay there. Someone, somewhere, prison authority—the higher-ups, whoever they are—decide. Or do they? The Bible declares in the book of Acts, *God determines the times and places of our habitation.* How much my movement after the Camp Hill riots was determined by the system and how much was the hand of God I'll leave to you to ponder. What I know is that He was with me every step of the way!

They woke me up, and it was time for another hurry-up-and-wait experience. They were shipping me off to Phoenix, Arizona, by way of Atlanta, Talladega, and El Reno—geographically, a head-scratcher of a trip, as only the efficiency of prison travel planners could organize.

Moving and transitions are always hard. As I entered into this phase of my journey, I wondered where Henry and Warner had wound up. *Had they gotten on buses? Were they still at Camp Hill? Would I see them again?*

And of course, the discomfort and mind-numbing sloth of it all—even the smallest steps take forever. Lists, process out, searches, chains, shackles, move the group from one place to the next, process in, and then do it all over again for the next leg of the trip. I'd been in long enough now that worries of what awaited me in the population of my new setting wasn't a big deal. I'd learned that if you just treat guys the way you want to be treated, it goes a long way.

They took 29 of us to the Federal Correctional Institute in Phoenix. I knew two of the other guys. But the place was a palace compared to the life we had at SCI Camp Hill. Maybe I should state that the other way around

... Camp Hill was a dump compared to this place! And inmates had so much more freedom here, were treated with more dignity and respect by COs. It was a night and day difference. All-in-all, this wasn't a bad landing site.

My first few days there, I ran around like a chicken, taking it all in. Then it occurred to me: *I am here to minister—I was a missionary to FCI Phoenix!* And that's what my time there would amount to ... ministry.

I got settled in. I got a good job and got involved in the church. Pastor Larry and his wife, Devi, flew out to see me. I was so thrilled—and so touched—that they'd made the 4,000-mile roundtrip journey. *Who does that?* These two dear people showed me God's love and compassion like nobody else. I wanted to live life that way—submitted to what God wants and directs, ready to go anywhere, anytime He leads, just to love someone with the love of Jesus!

Of course, Pastor Larry brought me encouragement. "You're not here by coincidence, Gene. Listen for His leading."

During one of my workouts in the yard, I saw a guy sitting on one of the weight benches, reading a small pocket-Bible. I walked his way.

"Hey brother, how you doing?"

He looked up, nodded, and smiled. "Is that a Bible?" I asked. "Are you a Christian?"

"I am," he replied.

I extended my hand and said, "Gene! My name is Gene." We shook hands.

"Frank!" he said.

Frank sported a crew-cut, had a bodybuilder's frame, and the dark tan of someone who spent a lot of time in the sun. He was from Montana originally, but had been living in Arizona while competing in bodybuilding tournaments.

He was arrested for dealing steroids, cocaine, and painkillers. I asked him, "Why painkillers?"

He explained it was easier to diet down for competition on pain meds. "I trained heavyweight, weighing 260 pounds, and then have to cut weight for competition. I'd lose 50 pounds, but I was shredded!"

I couldn't imagine it. He'd just started his 12-year sentence for dealing.

He asked me where I was from. When I told him Camp Hill, he said he'd seen news coverage of the riots. We both agreed, it was a wonder no one was killed. And I considered, again—*it wasn't a coincidence that I was here.*

Frank shared his testimony, how he'd come to faith. While detoxing in a federal psychiatric hospital in Missouri—the same place where disgraced televangelist Jim Bakker was housed—he was curled up in a ball, his body aching for drugs, and he cried out for help. "I cried out to Jesus," he said, "and just like that—immediately—my withdrawals ended. Jesus delivered me!" His was a powerful testimony.

We agreed that in the Scriptures, the Church was born when people got together and devoted themselves to prayer. So we planned to meet each night from 7 to 8 to pray, to see what God would do.

It was just the two of us at first. We read prayers from the Bible and prayed for revival in the prison. We started interceding for members of rival gangs in the prison, for Muslims, and for members of the Arian Brotherhood. Unlike my experience in Pennsylvania where blacks and whites and Hispanics hung out together, here there was very obvious separation. When you'd walk into the dining hall, you'd see it clear as day—this group here, that group there; each had its own section.

It wasn't long before the Lord began to add guys to our prayer meeting each night. Soon we were about 10 in number. One evening, an officer in charge of the yard approached. "I see you guys out here every night. Would you rather have a classroom in the Education Building?" he asked.

We were stunned. "Yes! Absolutely!"

Richard, one of the older brothers in our group, leaned over to me and said, "When does an officer ever offer help like that?"

Beginning the following night, we gathered in our own classroom. We took chairs and formed a circle. "Frank and I want to focus on praying for revival while we are here," I told the guys. "We want to pray for the lost, the sick, and for the administration and staff." Everyone agreed.

Soon our group was 25 men and growing. When we ran out of chairs, guys just kneeled on the floor as we prayed. We raised our hands, crying out for revival and for mercy, and for other inmates to come to know God better. Then one night I looked up and realized—there were even more guys standing at the windows, looking in as we prayed.

People were getting saved. They'd testify that they were just walking by and felt drawn to the room and what was happening inside. Others came and asked us to pray for them. They'd sit down and we'd lay hands on them and pray. It was very much like a second-chapter-of-Acts sort of experience. We all knew God was moving powerfully in our midst—and for that reason, we prayed all the harder expecting opposition from the enemy.

Then one day, word came down from above: Our group was no longer permitted to meet without the Chaplain present. I didn't understand, as we'd been meeting for six or eight weeks without any problem. I went to see the Chaplain to inquire.

"Gene, you and Frank never asked for my permission before starting your group," he said. It didn't make any sense to me. *Ask permission? We were just guys getting together to pray for others. How was this a bad thing?*

He wasn't going to budge. And the decision stood—we couldn't meet in the building anymore. So we moved our meeting back out to the yard.

But we also made a discovery where our attitude toward the Chaplain was concerned. We were offended and discouraged by his lack of support, and we allowed it to manifest in our speaking ill of him, as if he was an enemy. He was an authority—and God wasn't going to bless us in our rebellion. Conflict seemed to swirl until we realized we were in the wrong.

So we humbled ourselves, confessed our sin, and began to pray for and support the Chaplain. And God blessed that turn-around in our hearts. Our meetings continued my entire stay in Phoenix. Right up until the day a subpoena arrived.

I was headed back to Camp Hill.

It had been a year since the Camp Hill riots. And remember Albert—the guy who dove under my bed to hide? He had been pinched for arson somewhere in his past. Investigators charged him with starting fires during the riot. I was summoned to testify—perhaps provide an alibi that Albert couldn't have started them, as he was hiding in my cell.

Cue the process ... transport, search, chains, shackles ... and hours upon hours of travel.

During the trip, we stopped at El Reno in Oklahoma. They processed us in for the night. I was in a bullpen cell with like 60 guys. I was just trying to mind my own business, get through the evening, and get back underway.

"That damn Albert..." I heard someone say. I turned to look, and immediately recognized the speaker, a mountain of a man—Tony Mac, guys called him. You couldn't miss Tony. This guy squatted 800 pounds, bench-pressed 400. You can imagine: his muscles had muscles. Although Tony and I were at Camp Hill together, we'd never really spoken to one another before. I walked over.

"I had it so good in Fed," he said. I could relate. "That damn Albert, I don't even know him! What's he doing giving them my name?" We were both returning to Camp Hill for the same reason.

When we arrived at Camp Hill, they put Tony and me in a cell together for 30 days. He was a workout animal.

"Gene, let's do 500 pushups," he'd challenge me.

"I'm not doing no 500 pushups," I'd say.

"Let's go! Start counting!" He'd drop and do sets of 100, no sweat. I'd drop, grunt my way toward 40. We'd laugh.

One day—and I don't recall what prompted it—I offered Tony Mac the small Bible I had. "You interested in reading this?" I asked. He nodded.

I wrote a note in the front cover: "Read this Bible to be wise; Believe it to be safe; Apply it to be holy." I saw him reading that Bible often the rest of our time together.

Turns out my testimony didn't help Albert. He was in my cell on Friday— but needed an alibi for Thursday. It sure seemed to me like someone might have figured that out before summoning me back across the country. *Not a coincidence*, I told myself. *God's in this.*

One benefit of returning to Camp Hill was that I got to reconnect with Henry. Henry was one of the guys I'd really bonded with early on in my incarceration. I'd guess it was back in '81 or '82 when we met. It was out on the football field. Henry wasn't playing, but he was hanging around giving our quarterback advice. Good advice.

Henry was a handsome Italian guy, stood about 5'8" and weighed maybe 150 pounds. He had a full head of thick, black hair—looked like a model you'd see on the cover of *GQ*. And he was smart. He read a lot and was very well versed in any number of topics.

I don't think he'd mind me telling you, at that point in his life he was an expert in getting a hold of drugs and getting high. I was a willing co-conspirator. That's how we forged our initial bond—we were party buddies. But our friendship lasted beyond that phase. When I got into my relationship with Christ and Henry revisited his Catholic roots, our friendship deepened.

Henry had never left Camp Hill after the riots. He was among the small number of guys who remained. Their experience was pretty harrowing by all accounts. Inmates spent three days and nights outside in the elements—it took that long for crews to make one of the units livable again.

"They finally brought us in, 10 at a time," Henry explained. "They made us all strip for a search. The first thing you grabbed when they told you to get dressed—that was what you were leaving in, only one item. So, a guy grabs his t-shirt—that's it. A guy grabs boxers—you're done. Guys were walking around having turned their t-shirt into shorts, their legs through the arm holes." He told me they were then chained in pairs and put into cells. "So if one guy had to use the toilet, the other guy had to stand right next to him." It went on for several days until the ACLU came in and made the COs unchain the men. The picture he painted sounded brutal.

Henry's experience *was* brutal. "When we came in, one of the COs yelled, 'Hey, it's Scarfo.'" I remembered Scarfo—he was an Italian inmate with a bad reputation. He'd been seen on camera during the riots as an instigator. This CO's misrecognition cost Henry a beating.

"They started hitting me with their clubs. I just dropped and covered up." Henry said if it hadn't been for an older CO who saw what happened and came running to his aid, shouting, "That's not Scarfo!" he would have been seriously injured.

That's the sort of injustice that sometimes happens behind bars—stuff that never gets answered for. I understand the COs were angry, several of their friends had been hurt. I'd be mad, too. But treating people like this wasn't acceptable. Isn't acceptable. Ever.

Henry also informed me what happened to all my belongings—everyone's belongings—after the riots. We'd been told "Everything was lost." Indeed, it was—after crews swept everyone's possessions out of cells, into the hallways, they sent Bobcat tractors in to scoop the stuff into dumpsters. Everything I owned—a growing library of theological books, photo albums, personal letters, items I'd bought over the years—gone. Forever gone.

Henry got me a job in the laundry with him. We were back to spending a lot of time together. It was good; I'd missed his friendship over the year we were apart.

Eventually I was offered a better job in activities—they were in a rebuilding mode at Camp Hill, so setting up and overseeing activities was a posh job to have. I told them, "I'll take the job if Henry can come, too."

It wasn't all good, though. It was somewhere in that window of time that my second application for commutation was denied. Whereas I'd recognized my application wasn't that strong the first time through, this time I felt like I had a lot more going for me. I'd put another year in my sentence behind me. I was the only lifer chosen to participate in the vocational training building program. I'd participated in Prison Adjustment groups, volunteered with the Lifer's Association, served as a Chairman of their Project Committee—my resume was impressive.

I'd also taken part in a series of one-on-one sessions with the staff psychologist. The guy reminded me of pictures I'd seen in history books of General Ulysses Grant. He had stiff hair and a weathered face and beard. But he had a pretty warm personality and was easy to talk to.

During those talks, I would talk through the crime and share my remorse for it. I explained how my faith, my relationship with the Lord, had helped me take responsibility for my actions and allowed me to move forward, serving others.

He was very interested in the concept of discipleship as I shared with him the impression Pastor Larry had made on me. As Larry had invested in my life and mentored me over the years, I wanted to invest in and mentor others. I explained how important accountability is in the discipleship process. He nodded his head. I expected he was in full agreement with me. In all, we met for 12 weeks. I felt really positive about our interactions.

So understandably, I was devastated when this man I'd spent all that time with spoke against my application. "I believe Gene was a young follower at the time of his crime. If not for his cousin's influence, I don't believe he would have been involved," he began. "But I'm afraid he's still a follower. Now he follows this Pastor Larry, who may be a good man, but I believe Gene has yet to break the pattern of following others in his life."

My blood was starting to boil. I couldn't believe his words—his perspective. In all of our meetings, in all of his questions about discipleship, he'd never hinted that he thought it was a bad thing. This guy was going to roadblock my application! I prayed to remain calm. I tried to very gently explain my motives for discipleship, the concept of discipleship—that following a pastor who was helping me learn to follow after Jesus was not a bad thing, and rather a very good thing.

"Pastor Larry has mentored many men who've gone on to be leaders, pastors, missionaries," I said. "He's helped me discover God's calling on my life, to influence others to follow Jesus." *How could they misunderstand this?*

The committee decided, though, with the psychologist's reservations, they could not support my application. The process would move forward, but the reality remained: I knew my application was dead in the water. I walked back to my cell, knelt down, and gave thanks to God—for my salvation and for the Holy Spirit's power to cope with this disappointment.

A verse came to my mind, 2 Corinthians 5:17—*Therefore, if anyone is in Christ, he is a new creation; old things have passed away; behold, all things have become new.*

I was instantly reminded: *I am a new creation. I'm no longer that selfish guy who cares only about himself. I have a new identity now. I'm a son of God. A servant.* Pastor Larry told me many, many times in all our visits: "Servants don't have rights." I had no right, no entitlement, to expect the psychologist to support my application. Whatever feelings of rejection or offense I might harbor, they needed to go. I needed to let them go. I began praying for the staff psychologist—that he'd come to know Jesus, that he'd be blessed.

It was just a few weeks later that official word arrived: my application had been denied "for lack of institutional support." It was okay. I'd emotionally moved on.

And I'd physically move on, too—this time to SCI Rockview. And unbeknownst to me, I was headed for another reunion.

Another move meant another miserable transfer process. I wound up overnight at Smithfield, preparing the next day to ship to what would be my new, permanent address. I was lumped into a holding cell with eight or 10 guys. It was hot. We were crowded together. Guys had bad breath. They smelled. I was just thinking, *Lord, get me out of here!*

They opened the door for a few more guys to join us, and who walks in? Big Moses—Warner!

"I had a dream last night, Gene," he said. "The Lord told me I'd be seeing you today!"

It was a wonderful and welcome sight for me seeing Warner again. He had been in the Federal Institute in Terra Haute, Indiana. Now he was on his way ... with me ... to Rockview.

———————— ❧❀❧ ————————

When a year had passed since my last commutation try, I prepared to submit my next application. But the climate for commutation had changed pretty drastically, thanks to a guy named Reginald McFadden.

It was all over the news. McFadden was serving a life sentence for murder at the time of the Camp Hill riots. When the violence broke out, he helped protect an officer—outfitted him with a prison jumpsuit and helped him escape.

The Board of Pardons concluded, "This is the kind of inmate who deserves to have his sentence commuted." The Governor signed off. McFadden was released to live in a halfway house in New York City. Within just a couple of months, he was arrested again ... charged with rape and three more murders.

Commutations were hard to come by before—maybe a dozen or so a year at one point—down to just a handful. Now, with the political fallout and finger-pointing in the aftermath of the McFadden debacle, the door was all but nailed shut.

While it was certainly a discouraging development, I didn't lose sight of the fact that God was in this—ultimately my life was in His hands, not the hands of a Board of Pardons or the Governor. I rejoiced that I had a lot of people pulling for me.

Pastor Larry had gone so far as to send me a Pennsylvania Driver's Manual, saying, "When you get out, you'll need to get a license." He'd encourage me, "Picture yourself out, Gene. A free man—going to movies, having a job, sitting in a traffic jam."

Another great boost of encouragement arrived around that time— Henry was transferred in from Camp Hill. I'd missed him. It was great to be back together. I got him a job with me. We worked together. We worked out together. It was like old times again. He started attending the Catholic services at Rockview, but he also joined me for several Protestant services and programs. I could tell God was at work in Henry's heart. And I thanked Him for reuniting us, so I could be a part of encouraging Henry's faith.

I was learning, time and again, that nothing happens by coincidence. God orchestrates the pieces on His playing field. He moves you where He wants you to be; puts people in your path He wants you to meet and minister to. Ministry happens wherever and whenever you avail yourself of God's will. Another example—my friend Will.

Every Sunday morning, for several weeks in a row, I saw this guy sitting on a trash can down the end of our block. I'd be on my way to church and he'd be leaning back, with his feet up, reading something.

I always said, "Good morning! You want to come to church with me?" He'd politely decline. But I stayed after him. Week in and week out, I'd slow down, chat a little bit more, and extend the invitation. Will was his name, but guys called him "Surf."

I remembered how Pastor Larry had asked me, "What do you need?" when we'd met years earlier. The fact that he cared, his willingness to meet my needs, blessed me. And I'd learned how the littlest things can truly make a big difference. So in talking to Surf, I noticed he was dealing with some painful dry skin. One Sunday when I saw him, I dropped off a bottle of lotion I bought at the commissary for him.

Prison culture, you might imagine, often misinterprets kindness. If people give you stuff, they expect something in return. In fact, I'd given guys stuff over the years—sneakers, food, lotion, whatever—and guys accused me of being gay. I had to assure them I was just being a friend. No strings attached. No expectations.

One day, I looked up to see Surf walk into our Sunday School class. He sat down way in the back. He was writing letters or something, not really paying attention. That was fine with me. A couple weeks later, he moved a little closer. He was still writing, not participating. But then, he came a little closer still. Next thing I knew, Surf was sitting in the front row, a Bible open on his lap, participating.

We were talking one day about it. "You were the only guy who stopped by to talk," he said, recalling those Sunday mornings. "You gave me that lotion—a white guy, caring!" he laughed. "You know, I wondered if you were gay!" We both laughed.

"Thank you," he said.

"No. Thank the Lord," I told him. "God is good!"

I felt like I was sitting at the feet of the prophet that summer. Every morning I spent a couple of hours in the book of Jeremiah. It's a rich book in demonstrating God's relentless and faithful pursuit of His people, even to the lowest parts of society. So undoubtedly it spoke to my heart as an inmate: God hadn't—and wouldn't—forget or forsake me.

I was sharing my cell that summer with a man named Clyde. He was in his 60s and had been caught, a few too many times, driving drunk. I felt bad for him. He had to pace himself walking around. The trek upstairs on the range was sheer torture for him. He'd climb one flight of stairs and then lean on the rail for several minutes to catch his breath. *I'd hate to be old and in poor health, like that, in here...*

Clyde's struggle was on my mind one day as I finished up my reading and went out to the yard to exercise. I got in some lifting and ran a few laps and then took a seat on the wooden bleachers.

The yard was quiet that morning—not too much activity. I noticed a man walking my direction, from some distance away. I didn't know him personally, but I recognized him—his name was Kenny, a fellow lifer. I'd heard stories about him. He was given a life sentence for murder, and then, soon after he was incarcerated—more than 40 years ago now—he killed another inmate in self-defense. Kenny would never get out. He'd been here so long, he'd gained favor in the institution, and everyone liked him.

Kenny's walk was labored. He was hunched over, and it looked as if every step was painful. As he got closer, I noticed deep lines of aging etched in his face. His shoulders slouched as if they were caving under a heavy load. Those things together with his scraggly gray hair and beard made him look even older than he was. And he, too, like Clyde, was breathing heavy to walk the distance across the yard in the summer heat.

I spoke my thoughts out loud: "I don't want to grow old in prison ... and look like that!"

I was 37 at the time. I took better care of myself and worked out harder than most of the young guys. But I hated the thought that one day, that would be me. The sight of old Kenny left me overwhelmed with a sense of fear. I panicked. *I don't want to live in a geriatric unit with other prisoners having to feed me and bathe me. I don't want to die in here.*

They blew the whistle. Yard time was over. I took my gloomy thoughts and walked back to my cell. Clyde, my cellie, was a reminder of aging—I noticed the lines on his face, the hunch in his back, the limp in his walk—his struggles to cope. I felt a heaviness in my heart I hadn't felt before, like a dark cloud hung over me. Over the next couple of days, I even struggled to read and pray.

On the third morning, I sat with my Bible opened to Jeremiah and began to ponder just what the heaviness was; it seemed my life and ministry were shut down, crippled by fear. I cried out to the Lord. I prayed in the Spirit.

There are some 500 guys on the unit, so it's pretty loud in that place. But it was as if the place fell silent for me ... and I heard the Lord speak to my heart: "Go back into the yard; sit on those bleachers."

I made my way back to the same spot I'd been before. Confused about why I was there, I again cried out to God in prayer. As I did, I heard the Lord speak to my heart again. He said, "I want you to tell me you are afraid to grow old and die in prison."

I knew exactly what He wanted me to do—and why. I had not been trusting God with my entire life—or my death. Tears welled up in my eyes. I looked out across the yard, and everything and everyone was blurred. "Tell me," He said.

I struggled to form the words. I was so humbled and broken. I felt foolish. Finally, I whispered, "God, I'm afraid to grow old and die in prison."

I cannot express the feeling of relief simply admitting my fears to God brought. The tears poured down over my cheeks; a flood of His love and comfort, of His assurance and grace, washed over me. It was cleansing. Freeing. And it got better, still. I heard God say to me, "Ask me to take care of you." This time I didn't hesitate. I spoke the words out loud!

The heaviness on my heart completely disappeared. I looked out across the prison yard with a renewed purpose and tear-free vision—these people were reachable. They needed the Gospel.

A verse I'd memorized came to me: *The Spirit of the Lord is on me, because he has anointed me to proclaim good news to the poor. He has sent me to proclaim freedom for the prisoners and recovery of sight for the blind, to set the oppressed free.*

I walked into the activities office. Who was sitting behind the desk? Tony Mac! I hadn't seen him in years, since we were summoned back to Camp Hill together. Here he was at Rockview, a clerk in the activities department.

"Hey, Tony!" I shouted. "What are you doing, man?"

He looked up and smiled. "Reading."

He flipped back to the inside of the front cover and slid the little worn-out book he'd been holding toward me on the desk. "Check it out," he said.

"Read this Bible to be wise; Believe it to be safe; Apply it to be holy."

I'd forgotten I had given it to him years earlier. "I read it every day," he said. Tony had come to faith in Christ!

CHAPTER 12

DIVINE
APPOINTMENTS

S tarting each day in prayer was routine. It was so cold in the unit most mornings from the air conditioner going all night, I'd often lay, all bundled up under the covers to be warm, and raise my arms straight up into the air as I prayed—I must have been a sight!

I began each day thanking God for my life, for salvation, and for His purpose for me. In the early days of my faith, I followed a pretty regimented routine of prayer and reading the Word. After a few years of walking with the Lord, however, I became more comfortable submitting to the Holy Spirit's leading in my prayers—sensing who He'd have me pray for and how to pray for them. Sometimes His leading came prompted by a word of Scripture I'd read, or an experience during the day. Sometimes it was just a thought or impression that came to mind.

Twenty years. That's how long it had been since we'd exchanged letters last. Then as I was praying one morning, out of nowhere, Rob's face appeared in my mind, clear as day. Rob was a great friend during my middle school and high school years. We had a lot of classes together, we hung out how kids do. My incarceration at 17 put an abrupt end to that.

We lost touch for a few years. Rob graduated, enlisted, and went out west with the Navy. Somewhere in that timeframe, in the early 1980s, he became a Christian and started writing me letters—long, Jesus-saturated letters.

Rob wrote by hand on 10 sheets or so of long, yellow legal-pad paper, covered front and back, and full of Bible verses and stories about Jesus Christ. He always added in encouragements, like, "Following Jesus is the best decision

I ever made in my life" ... "God's given me peace and purpose in this life. He will do the same for you." He wrote out verses about salvation for me, and gave me references to others, encouraging me to look them up myself.

He shared things he was learning in Bible studies. He wrote about the way of salvation, "The Romans Road." There was a letter about prayer. Another argued Jesus is the Son of God.

It's a strange thing—my reaction. I loved receiving letters from him, and I read them over and over. It was so different from the kid I knew in school, this religious version of Rob. His excitement over his faith was genuine. I knew it. But it wasn't for me. I knew that, too.

I'm guessing he wrote to me for about a year. I quit replying. Eventually his letters stopped.

Looking back, it was another glimpse of light along my path. Here I was now—a believer, and 20 years down the road from Rob's letters—and his face appears to me as I'm praying. I began recalling the words, the lessons, the prayers he shared so long ago, and I was blessed with an occasion to thank the Lord for His reach into my life through Rob.

I didn't think much more about it until a month or two later. Again, while I was praying one day, there was Rob's face. I didn't know why this was happening, but sensed it was of the Lord. I began praying for Rob and, more specifically, that he and I might connect again after all these years. I began to pray that prayer often.

Maybe two months had passed when my sister, Mary, and her husband, Joe, surprised me with a visit.

I asked, "What's the special occasion that brings you out here?"

They'd just purchased a new truck and wanted to take a road trip to break it in. Joe suggested to Mary, "Let's go see Gene."

"There it is," Joe beamed with excitement. "I parked it in front of the window so you could see it."

And it was exciting. No one in my family had ever bought or drove a new vehicle before. We looked out the window—it was a beauty. Joe and Mary ran off a list of all its features. I was thrilled for them.

"Where did you buy it?" I asked.

"Oh, that's the cool part," he began. "We bought it from a friend of yours."

A friend? Who could it be? I'd been incarcerated for more than two decades.

"Your buddy, Rob," Joe said.

I was stunned!

I was thanking God, even as we talked. *Thank you, Lord! I'd seen his face and been praying to reconnect with Rob, and now this—out of the blue!*

I asked Joe and Mary, "How did you meet him?"

"We went to the hometown dealership and started talking to this salesman. He mentioned that he'd grown up in town and graduated from Tunkhannock High School. Then Mary said, 'I went to Tunkhannock; my maiden name is McGuire.'"

Rob didn't remember my sister. He told them, "I had a friend named Gene McGuire. You related?"

And Mary revealed, "That's my brother!"

Joe said, "He told us he's been thinking of you, and he wants to get back in touch—that it's been years since you guys had been in contact."

God is so good!

They explained that Rob was so excited for the chance to reconnect, he talked about inviting himself along on their road trip to see me. When he learned it's not that easy—that you have to be added to an inmate's visitors list, and you can't just show up—he got my contact information from Mary and promised he'd connect with me soon.

He did. We were exchanging letters that week, I added him to my list, and soon after he came to see me.

I was so thrilled to tell Rob about it—how his face had appeared in my mind as I prayed, and how I'd specifically asked the Lord to reconnect us. We were both blessed realizing how God had answered our prayers.

We reminisced over the letters we'd exchanged years earlier. He'd joined the Navy and got saved. That's when he started writing to me. We caught each other up over all the years. I was able to share with him my story of coming to faith in Jesus. He was so happy for me. And then he began telling me about a lot of our friends he was still in touch with—many of them were believers now, too. Rob helped fill in some of their stories and offered to help me reconnect with many of them.

"Bill's a believer now, too," he said. "In fact, he's on fire for God! Ministering..."

My jaw must have hit the floor! "Bill?!"

He was the star of our high school football team—the guy all the girls wanted to date and all the guys wanted to be. The friend whose mom invited us to church when we were kids—he was raised in a Christian home, but wasn't a believer himself. I knew that he'd been working in the Corrections Department for years, first in athletics and then as a drugs-and-alcohol counselor. But faith? Not Bill.

"It was pretty messy. Had something to do with alcohol. You'll have to hear it from Bill, himself," Rob said. "God used all that and some other stuff in his life to break through. Bill still works in the prison system, but now he's ministering for the Lord, too."

Alcohol? Bill never drank when we were in school. It was hard to imagine. But awesome to know—whatever it was, God has used it for good!

I had a flashback to the earliest days of my incarceration in juvie. I was out shooting some hoops, and I saw a line of cars pull into the faraway parking lot. I watched as a group of kids spilled out—they were looking my direction, but they were far enough away I couldn't make out if I knew them. Then I heard the officers call me: "McGuire, get in here!"

A week later, a letter came. "They turned us away," my friend Bill wrote. "Like 30 of us loaded up and drove over. They said you weren't allowed any visitors but family." That was Bill and a bunch of my friends from school that I had seen that day.

It was another 10 or so years later—this time when I was at Camp Hill— that I bumped into Bill. He was with Corrections, working in athletics, and his department brought some inmates over from another institution for some intramural sports events. It felt a little weird for me. Had to be really weird for him—he was prison staff, and his high school best friend a lifer. I knew they'd be watching us. I didn't want to do or say anything that would put him in an awkward position or cause him grief. But I did want to catch up. It was tough.

Many more years had passed. Rob promised to help me reconnect with Bill. And before long, the two of them visited me together. We indeed had a lot to catch up on. It was wonderful.

Bill introduced me to his wife, Karen, and two young daughters, Jordyn and Emily. His girls laughed and smiled—a true joy the entire visit. They all took an interest in the ministry I was involved in inside. I'd introduce guys to them, they'd get on visiting lists—within a couple of months, Bill was bringing a van of guys in to visit a bunch of guys I had the privilege of ministering to and investing in.

For the next several years, we ministered together like this—they'd come on Saturdays, a bunch of the guys and myself would meet them, we'd all eat hamburgers out of the vending machines, share, and fellowship. God is *so* good!

I am in awe of the way the Lord works—connecting the dots, maneuvering people into the right places, orchestrating circumstances, affording opportunities—all in the unfolding of His magnificent redemptive story. Sometimes His leading can start with a word during a sermon, or a vision during prayer.

And sometimes ... it just walks in the door and sits down.

I was sitting in my cell one evening watching a television program about the Bible. Orlando walked in and sat down next to me. I thought it more than a little awkward at first. While we knew each other and shared a few friends in common, we'd never really spoken much beyond greetings and pleasantries.

Orlando was maybe 15 years younger than me, of Puerto Rican heritage, from Philadelphia. He was doing a lot of time, 18 to 36 years. He was a model inmate, a well-intentioned guy, and very bright. I'd always see him going in and out of the Education Building or out in the yard, running the track.

To give you a glimpse into this guy's heart, I'll share one indelible memory I have of him...

The Lifer's Association hosted an annual Prison Run-a-Thon to raise money for Big Brothers and Big Sisters. One year, Orlando had trained very hard for the event, wanting to make a difference for the program. The morning of the race, he drank a bunch of pickle juice because he'd been told it reduced the chance of cramping. I don't know if he got any cramps, but by noon he was throwing up, sick as a dog!

You know what? He kept going! He fought on. He kept logging miles. By late afternoon, he was reduced to walking, but he didn't quit. He finished with 38 miles, and not even enough strength to walk back to the unit. Guys had to help him to the infirmary for an IV.

"Can I hang out and watch this with you?" he asked.

I nodded, and replied, "Sure."

The special was on the four gospels and the life of Jesus Christ. During the first commercial break, Orlando asked me some questions. I answered what I could.

Each commercial break offered us a little more time to dialogue. Orlando shared about his years of parochial school and how they'd never taught him who Jesus was. He was never encouraged to read the Bible.

When the show ended, we talked for another hour. I was super excited and wanted to try to lead him to the Lord right there, but the Holy Spirit told me to wait. I offered him a Bible, and he asked me where he should begin reading. I encouraged him, "Start reading the book of Philippians."

That was another God thing—I don't know why I said Philippians, but I felt like the Holy Spirit wanted Orlando to discover Jesus as a servant. I guess it's hard to get offended by someone whose motive is to serve you.

As Orlando left my cell, I prayed for him, anticipating, "Lord, what are you doing in his life? What part would you have me play?"

The next day Orlando came back, excited about what he'd read. This was a pattern that played out over several days. We'd talk over passages. He had many questions. I answered what I could. When he got to the end of Philippians, I encouraged him to go on and read Colossians. Again, for no other reason than the Lord laid it on my heart that Orlando needed to see the supremacy of Christ now, and that is Colossians' message.

Then one day Orlando showed up and said, "Gene, I did something I've never done before—I prayed!"

"What did you pray?" I asked.

He looked at me very seriously and said, "I prayed, 'Jesus, save me. I'm a nut!'"

I laughed out loud. He didn't.

"I'm serious!" he insisted. I knew he was, I was just overwhelmed by his honesty and simplicity.

I assured him, "God heard and answered your prayer, brother!"

Orlando wiped away tears as he described sitting in his cell and reading the Bible, the feelings that came over him, recognizing his life was out of control, and he just cried out from the heart. He told me God was already at work changing his life.

He threw out all his porn. He was supposed to purchase something illegally that afternoon and had a change of heart. "Called it off," he said, "I've been born again!"

I don't recall many guys as hungry and teachable as Orlando. We met for the next month or so, for two hours every night in my cell, reading and studying the Word together.

That was no small miracle—rules prohibited it. When one guy was going into another guy's cell, it wasn't good—it was to fight, steal, or have sexual contact—it wasn't allowed. But in all our time together, officers never interrupted us. Once an officer on rounds saw us, began to reprimand us until he saw our Bibles. And he said, "Sorry, Gene, you guys go on with what you're doing." Our get-togethers were a joy and a privilege for me, and a blessing to Orlando. God's favor was upon us.

I introduced Orlando to all the other brothers, inmates who were believers, and they were all encouraged by his salvation story. I also gave Pastor Larry a call, and he arranged a visitor for Orlando, a man named Mike who was a worship leader at his church and willing to travel the three-hours-each-way trip with Pastor Larry to see us.

Orlando had been a believer a few months when he came to me one day, tremendously disappointed, and said, "My cellmate made me use profanity!"

I thought for a second and replied, "He didn't make you use profanity, Orlando, that was already in you. It surfaced when you got mad."

He wrinkled his brow at my answer. I thought he might just curse at *me*!

"Shut up, Gene!" was all he said. He walked away angry.

We didn't speak for several days. Finally, he came back around and apologized. I explained to him that this was a lesson God was teaching me—when it comes to anger, it comes from two places: past wounds I've never forgiven and allowed to heal. and entitlements—things I think I deserve. I told him how this realization was changing my life! He took it to heart. Orlando is one of the most teachable young men I've ever worked with over the years.

God was really blessing the ministry at Rockview. The pastor had given some invitations—guys were coming forward and putting their faith in Jesus. With so many new believers, I knew discipleship was a crucial need. For all these years, Pastor Larry had been pouring his life into mine—visiting once a week way back at the beginning in Camp Hill, once a month ever since I'd been at Rockview, all the calls in-between visits—I knew this sort of investment was needed for all the guys to grow in their faith. Someone needed to help them process this newfound faith and commitment they'd made. Someone needed to help them find answers to their questions, find application for the lessons they'd learn, like Larry had with me.

Warner, Orlando, and I talked about it. We went to see Pastor Reitz and proposed we start a New Believer's Bible Study. He said, "Sounds like a great idea."

He even gave us permission to use his office. We met for an hour and a half every Sunday, with maybe eight or 10 guys. We talked about vital topics, prayer, confession, how to read the Word—and addressed questions they raised. I typed up discussion topics and questions. We spent the first part of our meetings covering that material, then we spent time sharing and praying together. It was awesome. And it was fruitful—guys were growing!

We organized things into 10-week cycles in order to move one group of guys through and make room for more. Those who graduated wanted to come back—they didn't want their involvement in the group to end. In my mind, that was a good problem to have! And things went on this way for about five years. It became a real highlight of my ministry.

Then one day, without any warning at all, the pastor called me into his office.

"Gene, I want you to step aside. I want you to give up leadership of the New Believer's Bible Study to Warner."

My first thought was: *No way! This is my baby! I love it!*

The only explanation he offered was, "I have my reasons." *What was that?* He wasn't leaving any room for discussion. The decision was made.

I walked back to my cell, whining all the way. I was angry. I felt like I'd been rejected, kicked to the curb, and without even so much as an explanation why. It's a terrible feeling. I cried out to God in prayer. *How is this your plan?*

God didn't give me a reason, but a funny thing happened as I was praying.

I started to realize that Warner would be able to offer "my guys" in the study group more than I could. Just as he'd always been a mentor and example to me, he was uniquely gifted and positioned to do more for them. It's as if God reminded me: 'What your heart really desires, Gene, is the very best for those guys.'

Maybe this was, indeed, a God thing! My heart started to come around.

A couple weeks later, after I'd embraced the change, the pastor asked me to start a weekly prayer meeting. I agreed. Every Tuesday morning we met—we prayed, some guys aloud, some guys silently, some in groups, some individually, sometimes over a specific list of prayer concerns, sometimes over items that just came up.

We started with a few guys. Word got out. Pretty soon it was a hundred. Not long after, it was 200! Two-thirds of the church came together every week to pray!

Now let's stop to imagine such a thing...

Say you live in a neighborhood near a corrections facility—and there are a couple hundred men in there ... gathering to *pray*! God had given me an even greater blessing in ministry.

Opportunities for me to share my story multiplied as well. Around 2002, the institution asked me if I'd be willing to meet with groups of high school students. I learned the Superintendent had, himself, requested my participation.

"Can I speak about my faith in Jesus?" I asked. My faith was, after all, the heart of my prison story.

The staff said yes. *Count me in.* And over the next decade, I'd talk dozens of times to high school and college students and rehab groups.

The high school groups were brought in as part of an awareness program. Students were assembled in the visiting area, officers and administrators gave them a brief talk on the prison and its programs. Then they'd bring me in—a real prisoner in a brown jumper, marked AK4192.

"This is Gene McGuire," they'd say. "He's serving a life sentence for murder."

A hush would fall over the kids. I'd share a little about my past, a little about prison life, and as much as I could work in about my faith in Jesus Christ before I finished.

Occasionally a group would arrive with a wise-guy, class-clown-type mixed in. They were easy to spot—I'd played that role myself once upon a different time.

I remember one kid tried to cop a laugh with a flippant comment, asking, "Hey, do you have to worry about the Russian Mafia in here?"

I didn't laugh. The group of students held their breath as I walked toward him. I looked him straight in the eye and calmly asked, "Do you think this is a joke?"

You could have heard a pin drop. "I put on this uniform every day. I'll be incarcerated for the rest of my life. I'm not leaving here. Ever. Is that funny to you? It's not to me. It sucks. There's no glory in this, my young friend!"

Funny boy didn't open his mouth again. I'd made my point, and quite an impression.

Sessions with rehab groups were a little more sobering—no pun intended. The struggles these folks were going through hit home for me. I was able to feel their pain, empathize with their situations—my own past with alcohol and drugs and my family history allowed me to relate. I shared a lot of my own experience, and it connected me to them. I could tell God was using these occasions, and my past, in people's lives. I gave thanks that He would use my pain.

The opportunities to meet with college students from Penn State University—Rehabilitation and Criminal Justice students—were quite different. Since they were adults studying for a future that might have them working in Corrections or with offenders, they were allowed into the prison, beyond the visitation room, into our auditorium. The setting afforded more time, an open format, a lot of dialogue, questions and answers, interaction. I met some really sharp young people through that program. I hope I left an unforgettable impression on them—the impression that Jesus was the Answer ... their Answer.

Just to reiterate: With God the process is as important as calling and anointing. These years of sharing my story, my testimony, interacting with the students—I couldn't have known at the time—was all part of preparing me for the future; part of God's process in my life.

One April afternoon, Mom came for a visit. Cancer had taken its toll. She'd gone through surgery, the chemotherapy—she was so thin, looked weak. But she was happy. She was praising the Lord! Our visit was wonderful. We talked over her involvement in her church, my ministry opportunities. We agreed: for all we'd been through, God had been so good to us! I hated to see her leave that day. I was thankful as I walked back to my unit.

It was just a month later, a May afternoon, when a counselor walked into the room where I was talking with some friends and said, "Gene, they asked me to tell you to give your nephew a call. It's important."

I excused myself and went straight to the phone.

"Hey, Uncle Gene," my nephew answered. "I don't know how to tell you this ... Grandma just died."

And that's how I found out. I walked back to the guys I'd been with before the call. The counselor had filled them in. They all knew my mom. They knew this was a blow. My friends waited with open arms and comforted me.

Rules had long ago changed—I wouldn't be able to go to her funeral as I had been allowed to attend my dad's more than a quarter-century earlier. I was remarkably at peace, though, knowing she was with the Lord, and that death wouldn't have the last word. I knew (and know) I'd see her again. My tears were a mixture of pain and joy.

<hr/>

A couple more years passed, and I filed my fifth attempt at commutation.

It had been more than seven years since I last filed. I was so very hopeful going in—I'd been incarcerated for more than 30 years. I had a lengthy resumé that now included several years of speaking to students at the invitation of the Warden; I'd served as President of the Lifer's Association; participated for years in the Association's benevolent and charity work; I had no opposition whatsoever from within the institution—in fact, I had a ton of support. My file contained a long and impressive list of what I'd done and an even longer list of important people in my corner.

As always, the process included waiting. And more waiting. Your mind plays tricks, too, always tricks. In one instant, you think the longer things take it could mean good news. The next, you're certain the long wait means your paperwork fell into some administrative abyss somewhere. This time around it took 2-and-a half years for me to hear.

Word came from the Deputy Superintendent: I'd been denied again. Oh, it hurt! No matter how hard I tried to protect myself, prepare myself ... *denial hurt*. And this time, all the more, because everyone really believed—I really believed—I had a good shot.

Like all the denials before, the aftermath was really tough. So many people knew and were waiting anxiously to hear the news. Having to tell them all I'd been denied again was like adding insult to injury. So painful. I'd have to let folks know. But first, I'd have to come to grips with the news myself.

I walked back to my cell without talking to anyone. I collapsed to my knees next to my bunk and cried. Immediately I heard the Lord say, "Thank me." And I did.

I gave Him thanks—for His provision, for His protection, and even for His providence where this denial was concerned. A long list of occasions crossed my mind, years' and years' worth of situations when I recognized His hand upon me, directing my path, orchestrating circumstances for my benefit. Jobs I'd had in the prison; the platform to minister to and share with others; out-of-the-blue opportunities—from having met Senators Heinz and Specter to talk about jail overcrowding to being interviewed for the television program *Dateline*; meeting Sister Helen Prejean, the author of *Dead Man Walking*; having been chosen and included in Howard Zehr's book *Doing Life: Reflections of Men and Women Serving Life Sentences*.

It was crazy when I took inventory of it all. God was with me all along! I couldn't believe this situation was any different—I couldn't see how, but I'd trust: He was in this, too!

I cried. I prayed. I confessed my hurt and confusion. I professed my trust in Him. And then I heard it—clear as day—God's voice: "I will release you, Gene!" And He clarified, "It's not going to be based on what you've done or who you know—I'm going to release you!"

I stood up, brushed away the tears and went back to work, back to worship, back to meeting with the brothers in the yard, back to witnessing to and praying for my fellow inmates. That's what He'd called me to do. That's what I did.

I had no idea when or how, but I knew with absolute certainty ... He would release me.

CHAPTER 13

MAIL CALL

Two months or so passed. It was June 2010. I received a letter from an attorney named Bridge—I believe he was working in cooperation with the organization Fight for Lifers, which advocates on behalf of inmates serving life sentences without the possibility of parole. We always got stuff from this organization—updates on legislation and information on changes in the system.

It was an ongoing battle. Inmates wrote legislation and tried to get politicians to push it through. There was fighting over verbiage.

To give you an idea: Someone proposed a plan where guys sentenced for first-degree murder could be eligible for parole after serving 30 years, and guys sentenced for second-degree could be eligible after 25. But guys argued it wasn't fair. There were some who'd actually committed the crime who got second- or third-degree, while guys who didn't might have pleaded out to first-degree. Around and around it went.

Honestly, I didn't put much stock in any of it. For me, my freedom wasn't happening this way. Commutation was my only hope. I wouldn't get any relief from legislation or the courts.

This letter was different. It was legal mail. I never got legal mail unless it was from the Board of Pardons denying my commutation. The COs called me over to the desk and opened it in front of me—it was a Post Conviction Relief Act Petition. It had something to do with a recent Supreme Court decision, *Graham v. FL*, and its impact on juveniles sentenced to life without the possibility of parole.

I took the papers and walked back to my cell. There was quickly a buzz circulating. I wasn't the only one who had received it. I had four or five other lifers in my unit, and there were maybe 200 throughout the institution.

A bunch of guys came to see me, wondering, "Are you going to file it, Gene?"

I told them I'd work on it. But the truth is, I wasn't planning to. After my last attempt at commutation was denied, and clearly hearing the Lord say, "I am going to release you," I really didn't think it would be through the courts. It didn't seem like an option for me since I never had a trial, and hadn't pursued appeals. I had no legal knowledge and no money to hire attorneys. I didn't believe there were any grounds to go back to court—so the paperwork sat on my desk, untouched.

To make matters worse, guys around me were filing their petitions and were hearing back—a big fat NO. My friend Jackie in the next cell—having already served about 40 years of his sentence—got his denial complete with a nasty note from the court—something like, "This court sentenced you to life, and you'll die in that prison!"

Other guys were getting similar replies. All the more reason, I concluded, not to bother.

The more I thought about it, though, the more I realized I had no opposition. Even the DA had written a supportive letter on my behalf. I had strong support within the institution, and a huge amount of support outside.

I'd been living by the belief that where there is peace in the decision-making process, it's probably God's will. So as the days were winding down—I think there was a window of 60 days from receipt of the letter to the filing of the petition—I began to pray over the envelope on my desk—and God gave me peace about it.

I filled out the paperwork with only a few days to spare. I gathered all of the information needed—docket numbers, attorneys' names, dates. I sealed it up and mailed it.

One week later I received a reply. I braced myself for a reply like Jackie's.

I opened the envelope and saw one word stamped across the document: GRANTED! The guys went wild with excitement for me. Everyone else had been denied. I'd have a hearing at least. This was big. *This was huge!*

A September date was set in Wyoming County. But panic set it. I'm not kidding. *What do I do now? I'm going back to court?* I can't really explain it, but my mind flashed through the realities—*I'd been in the same place for so long. This was home. This was life.* And thoughts of the process itself were overwhelming—leaving here, back to County, back and forth, meetings with attorneys...

How bizarre is that? I was potentially looking at a path out, and all I could think initially was how uncomfortable that path might be!

I was contacted by an attorney named Buttner out of Scranton. He said he'd been appointed to represent me. His first words of advice to me were, "Relax. This is going to take some time."

I don't know if I laughed out loud or not, but that sure was funny to me. *I'm a lifer! I've got time.*

He needed time, he explained, to bring himself up to speed on this *Graham v. FL* Supreme Court ruling, and then to immerse himself in my case. He said the September date was unrealistic and would need to be postponed. None of it really registered with me.

September became October. Then November. The hearing was rescheduled several times. And the strange thing? I wasn't discouraged by the delays. I still didn't think this would end in my release. Plus, I was living my life here. I had a growing ministry, a great job, dear friends, good relationships.

If a total uprooting of my life got delayed another month or so ... okay.

A few months had passed. I got an urgent message to call my attorney.

He said, "Gene, guess what we found?" *Obviously I didn't have a clue.* "We found your original attorney's files!"

The man had passed away several years earlier. His wife boxed up all his files and papers and delivered them to the county. They didn't know what to do with them. Someone apparently found a quiet, dark corner in the basement of the county jail to store them.

What irony: All these years I was doing time, and so were my records! I didn't know what it meant or why it was so important to him, but he viewed this find as a gold mine.

Then he peppered me with questions. "What did your attorney tell you? ... How much did you know?"

I wasn't sure where any of it was going, but I could tell his mind was moving a hundred miles an hour. It sounded significant.

Before we hung up, Mr. Buttner said, "Gene, you didn't have an adequate defense."

I continued living my normal routine. Guys were coming up to me asking, "What did you do?" since all the other requests had been denied. *How was it that my petition was granted?* All I knew to say was that this lawyer said my original lawyer provided inadequate counsel.

In the coming days, I got several letters from Mr. Buttner, and I was on the phone with him—a LOT—far more contact than I'd ever had with my original attorney. I suppose that alone was eye-opening for me.

A court date was finally set for September 2011.

As I'd anticipated, the rigors of it all set in. They had me move all my possessions into Reception and Discharge (R&D) at SCI Rockview. They put me in a holding cell over night with the other guys being transported the next day.

Morning came—they count us, process us out, line us up, shackle us together, out to the van, count us again, drive ... arrive, line us up, count us again, process us in, get us settled into holding cells. An all-day ordeal. Welcome to SCI Dallas.

Since Dallas wasn't my home institution, they'd house me—and all the guys being transferred—in isolation cells. In the Hole. No Bible. No papers. No nothing. I enjoyed all the hospitality a bare cell could offer for a couple of days before they moved me again. This time, a couple of sheriffs picked me up to take me to County, the jail a block from the courthouse where my hearing was scheduled.

The morning of they came to get me. Picture it: I'm dressed in an orange jumpsuit, shackled and cuffed, and a pair of officers walks me right down the middle of the street, one block from the jail to the courthouse.

I wonder what the neighbors must have been thinking while they were out getting the morning newspaper, sipping their coffee, walking their dog ... a group of high school girls running cross country going by ... and here goes a prisoner in shackles. *Do I say, "Good morning!"? Shout, "Stay in school, kids!"? Do I keep to myself?*

When I got to the courtroom, I saw Mary and a few of my friends. I nodded to them. I really had no idea what to expect. I suppose the thought of court led me to believe I might have to rehash the whole story. My attorney prepped me for what would happen: "I'll put you up on the stand and ask you a few questions. Then the DA will ask you a few questions. That's it."

He briefly tried to explain the legalities, or what was being considered by the court. This hearing was to determine whether or not my original attorney had led me into an illegal plea agreement. He had convinced me all those years ago to believe that by pleading guilty, the court could find me guilty of second-degree murder, or something less, like manslaughter. Which wasn't true. So this hearing was for the court to reconsider that original plea deal and, at the same time, to determine whether or not I received ineffective counsel.

I took the stand. Mr. Buttner asked me a few questions concerning my relationship with my original attorney.

"How many times did you see him?"

"I think it was three."

"How many times did you talk to him on the telephone?"

"Maybe twice."

"What did you believe would happen in court?"

"I believed the court would determine whether I was guilty of murder or manslaughter."

I knew the DA would question me next. As my attorney was speaking, I looked at him sitting at his table. He never looked up. He was writing on a legal pad—he looked totally disengaged to what was going on. It was disconcerting. I was expecting him to be the adversary here. I expected that whatever my attorney would argue *for* me, this man would argue *against*. *Aren't those the standard roles?*

When it was his turn, the DA looked up and said, "Good morning, Mr. McGuire." *Trick? He's being nice, and now he's going to get ugly, right?*

But I was astounded. The DA began asking me questions about my time in prison. He had my resumé in front of him. He wanted to know what I'd done to live on Honor Block. He asked about the education I'd received. He asked about the ministries I led, the committees I'd chaired, the charities I'd served. He asked me about the groups of high school students I'd spoken to and the interview I'd done with *Dateline*.

As he asked me those questions, and I rehearsed my resumé and all I'd been blessed to be involved in, it dawned on me—I hadn't wasted the years. *This was my life. And I had lived it.*

Then reality struck me—the DA wasn't my adversary. He was helping my cause! I was so thankful to God; I just couldn't believe this was happening.

He finished his questions, and the judge then said, "I have a question for Eugene."

He looked at me and asked, "Mr. McGuire, did you believe you could get a life sentence?"

I answered, "Yes, your Honor."

"Thank you," he replied, and looked down, making notes on the paperwork before him.

I wanted to say more. That wasn't the full answer. I called out, "Your Honor, may I say something else?"

"No!" he replied, sternly. It felt like a punch, like the wind was knocked out of me. *Did I just mess it all up?*

When I got back to my seat, my attorney whispered to me, "What was that?"

I whispered back, "I wanted him to know that I also believed I could get less than a life sentence." He assured me the judge knew that.

There was a little more housecleaning talk. Something about 60 days. Or 90 days. I had no idea what it was about. It occurred to me later: it was my life they were talking about, and I was just there like a fly on the wall. Strange phenomena.

When the hearing was over, my attorney told me, "Now we wait." He had no idea how accustomed to that reality I was.

They took me back to SCI Dallas. In my mind, I would be headed home to SCI Rockview, and the sooner the better. They had buses come and go. I was just waiting for them to call me for my bus. But the call didn't come. I was sitting in that isolation cell for days. I kept asking, "Sarge, am I on today's bus?"

"No, McGuire."

I was getting angry. There was absolutely no reason for me to be stuck here. I was suffering—no Bible, no books, no papers, about half the food I'm used to eating. They don't make the Hole comfortable for guys. More "Up all night, sleep all day." It's misery. I tried to keep my sanity, working out in my cell, doing pushups, trying to remember Bible verses, praying.

A few weeks went by—still no bus. I was beside myself. Frustrated. This temporary transfer meant being in holding, not in population. Trying to remember verses. Praying. Some letters. Going through it. Up all night, sleep all day.

Then a counselor came to see me. He introduced himself by saying, "Gene, I'm your cousin Bobby's counselor. He's asked if we could set up a meeting for the two of you. Are you willing to see him?"

I was stunned. I knew Bobby was at SCI Dallas. I'd asked a few of the guys who came to the Hole, "Do you know Bobby Lobman?"

Somebody would say, "Yeah, Jersey Bob—I know that guy."

Another one said, "That dude works out all the time."

So ... they knew him. I told guys, "Tell him his cousin Gene says hello."

The counselor explained that there were still some hurdles to cross. Nothing like this had ever been done before. But if all the powers-that-be signed off on it, they'd get us together.

My mind went to work. I was tripping out. *What did Bobby want? What would we talk about? Was he mad at me? Did he want to lash out at me? Hurt me? That was foolish. There wasn't bad blood between us. Maybe he'd want to say in person what he'd written to me more than a decade earlier:*

April 28, 2000
Dear Eugene,
    This is not an easy task for me. In the last 23 years I've never been able to get past the guilt I feel over destroying your life. It's easy to say that we all make our own decisions. But the truth is, we both know that if it hadn't been me, you would not have followed anyone else to that bar.
    I would give my life to change your situation. The bright side is your letter has assured me you have at least found peace in your spiritual growth. In the two days since I received your letter it's occurred to me that your decision to write me just may be God's way through divine intervention to help me get past the guilt and sadness I feel over your situation.

He went on in that letter to converse about "prison stuff"—how he'd had more years added to his sentence and how he wanted to stop all his violent behavior; he "prayed that circumstances never arise where I have to hurt another human being in any manner." He signed it, as I recall, "Take care, stay safe, and may God bless. Love, Bobby."

Perhaps he needed a catharsis—a coming clean. Something like he wrote in a second letter to me, a few months after the first:

July 18, 2000
Dear Gene,
     Writing to you isn't easy. The combination of guilt and sadness always causes me a profound melancholy. The unfairness of you still being incarcerated.
     I would like to know the next time you put in for commutation. I want to write a letter to the board explaining that if not for me you would not be in the situation you are in.
     If they look at my prison record they would see I've gotten an additional life sentence plus 80 more years in jailhouse cases. It would be easy to understand what a bad influence I was on you.

Or maybe it was just a profound desire to connect with family of some kind. The rest of that July letter painted a picture of real family turmoil in the wake of his crimes, punishment, and being out of their lives:

     I don't hear from the family at all. [My son] has his own life now. As long as he is happy and staying out of trouble, I'm happy for him. I love him very much, but I also have to respect his decision. Even if it is to extricate me from his life.
     In the last 15 years I hear from Arlene only when there are problems. 6 months ago she writes and tells me she has to come see me.

When she comes, she tells me [my daughter] is
using crack and living with a dealer. She tells
me the grand kids are in danger but she can't
do anything.

I was nominated to be the bad parent. So
I wrote all the agencies, even the attorney
general. I think they took the kids, last
I heard. But it seems Arlene used me. She
intentionally drew me into this knowing [my
daughter] would run to her for support, and
hate on me. I can accept my daughter hating me
forever for trying to get my grandchildren out
of that environment, but Arlene manipulating
me for her own selfish purposes—it's beyond my
ability to understand or forgive.

And he obviously wrestled to put it all in perspective:

The games people play still amaze me after
all these years. Psychiatrists diagnose me as
a sociopath. I don't even try to explain the
love I feel for my family. Or the guilt I feel
over the harm I've done in this lifetime. I've
reached a point where what others think of me
is a lot less important than what I think of
myself.

Curiously, he closed that letter with this:

As you know there is a higher power that will
judge us. And he knows what's in our hearts.

They shackled me and brought me into a secured area. There they had two cages against a wall—not much bigger than a man could stand up in. They put me inside and had me poke my hands out of the bars so they could remove the hand-irons from my wrists. A few minutes later, I heard a door open, and saw an officer and an inmate coming toward me.

I hadn't seen Bobby in more than 30 years. I didn't recognize him at first. He looked old—shoot, we were both old! He had this sort of gangster swagger about his walk. Our eyes met.

"Hey, Eugene." They started to put him in his cage, freeing his hands as they had mine.

"Hey, Bobby."

He began with an apology—much like he'd written all those years ago. It meant more to me, though, to hear him say it, to be able to look into his eyes.

"I'm so sorry for ruining your life."

I'd never really thought about it from his perspective before. I could tell it was a heavy weight he had carried all these years. My heart was filled with compassion for him.

"I'm sorry, too," I replied. "And you didn't ruin my life. I haven't wasted it."

He said, "Yes, I've heard. I've kept track of you over the years."

It made perfect sense. Bobby knew so many guys, knew the system. He was in touch with my sister for a while. And then after he'd messed that up, he kept tabs through others. He was a hustling guy—always had ways to hear, to know.

"I had open heart surgery," he said. "Those bastards saved my life— probably added on another five or 10. Should have just let me die." I couldn't tell if he was joking or serious.

"I'm tired of killing people, Gene." The two COs keeping an eye on us giggled. I wasn't sure if they thought he was being funny, or if what he said was funny.

"And Sid—I don't want to kill that motherf... anymore." The officers laughed again.

He continued, "You know that he's the one that told me about that place, that the old lady had a lot of cash. He's an idiot. Not worth it."

We talked about family. Another decade had passed since his letter, but it seemed like his relationships with his wife and kids—and grandkids—were still a rollercoaster. His daughter had been in touch, had come to visit. He seemed to want to move off that topic.

He mentioned that he'd not been in touch with my sister in quite some time. Something about how he'd gotten mad over the phone and threatened her and her husband. They'd had enough. He felt bad about it. Wished he could take it back.

He mentioned my mom. He missed her. He loved her. Felt terrible about all he'd put her through. I was able to tell him about the great healing we'd had in our relationship—a testimony of God's goodness. He seemed to bristle a little at that, the notion that I could say God was good to us even in spite of all we'd been through.

The officers told us to wrap it up. They let Bobby out first and went to work on his irons and shackles. We just stared at each other. They let me out, and before they shackled me they let us embrace.

Bobby said, "I love you, Gene," and gave me a kiss on the cheek.

"I love you, Bobby."

And that was it. They walked us out of the secured area, Bobby to his unit and me back to the Hole.

I wasn't back in my isolated cell 10 minutes when the Sergeant walked up and said, "Gene, I just heard. You're on the bus to SCI Rockview tomorrow."

I thought back through the several weeks I'd been forced to rot down here in Dallas, and it hit me—*the process!*

In God's economy, the process is always important. Yes, it was miserable, a real struggle all those weeks in the Hole. But had I not been there, gone through it, I wouldn't have had the opportunity to see Bobby. *God does know what He's doing! God is good!* And I cried tears of thankfulness and joy.

It was finally time to leave Dallas, to head home. The process again, search, change, paperwork (this time I had a box of paperwork with me for court, which I had to carry everywhere), then shackles and to the van.

On the way, we had to climb down a steep set of stairs, me in chains and carrying this box. An older officer behind me held onto the chain around my waist as we started down. I missed a stair—that's all I can figure. Head over heels, I bounced down the staircase. When I hit the bottom, I knew I was hurt—my shoulder was killing me—but I also knew that if I needed medical attention, I wouldn't be leaving. *My bus was waiting, and I was going to be on it!*

They asked, "You okay? You need medical?"

I shook my head. "I'm good."

They helped me get up, gather my things, the whole time looking me over.

"You sure you're all right?" *Get me out of here* was all I could think.

It felt great to be back home at Rockview. The guys saw me coming—I must have been a sight. I had lost 20 or so pounds in the month I was away. I had some fresh bumps and bruises from my header down the stairs.

"What the hell did they do to you?" the guys were asking.

They started forcing Chichis made from Ramen noodle soup into me. "You gotta eat something, man!" It was good to be home. Everybody wanted to know what happened in court and what was next. I didn't really know.

A few months later I got another letter. This one contained the DA's post-hearing brief. I read it—my heart leapt. He documented his findings. He'd spoken to the original prosecutor and detectives who were now all retired. He'd spoken to family members of the victim. He included letters from several people who supported me. Then he listed his conclusions:

```
Based on the above, the undersigned
prosecutor believes the following are true:
The defendant...
   • Did not murder Isabelle Nagy
   • Did not conspire to kill Ms. Nagy
   • Did not intend that Ms. Nagy be killed
   • Was not present inside the tavern when
     Robert Lobman killed Ms. Nagy
   • After hearing a loud noise and entering
     the tavern, told Robert Lobman to stop
   • Did not hatch the plan to steal money
     from the tavern
   • Was led along into the plan by his
     24-year-old cousin from New Jersey
   • Was unaware that his cousin was capable
     of the killing
   • Was under the influence of alcohol
```

That's only the first half of the list! It went on and on. Next, he detailed my accomplishments in prison—how I'd been a model inmate, been asked to serve on special prison committees ... again, all the things that reminded me my years hadn't been wasted.

The DA wrapped his brief up with the facts, followed by his recommendation:

```
The defendant has been incarcerated since he
was 17 years old. He's been incarcerated for
34 years. He's now almost 52. A life sentence
for a 17-year-old is substantially longer
than for someone who begins imprisonment in
mid-life.

The purpose of the criminal justice system—
punishment, deterrence, protection of
the community and rehabilitation of the
offender—would be fulfilled by accepting this
defendant's guilty plea to a charge of 3rd-
degree murder and resentencing the defendant
to the maximum term of imprisonment equal
to the amount of time the defendant has
presently served.
```

For the first time, I allowed myself to believe something good could come of this!

From that point, I started losing sleep. My imagination ran wild. *What would it be like to be free?* I thought about going home. Going by my old school. Walking around town. Looking up old friends. Starting a church. *Might I finally stand outside under the night sky again?*

I heard from my attorney next. He was hoping to have the judge vacate my sentence and re-sentence me. He used the words "parole-able sentence." That suggested there was a light at the end of the tunnel. How long the rest of the tunnel was—in years—didn't really matter to me. He thought the court might order me to serve a little longer and then transition to a halfway house or something similar. Again, all of it sounded fine.

After these conversations, I went to work daydreaming on halfway houses. *Which ones were good ones? Which ones were bad?* Wherever I landed I knew I'd be ministering. *Maybe I should choose a bad one. Perhaps God had a plan for me to reach guys in a really bad place.* My imagination ran non-stop.

Then came a package in the mail that I couldn't have imagined...

ORDER
    AND NOW, this 9th day of February, 2012, upon consideration of Defendant's Petition for Post Conviction Relief Act Appeal, the brief(s) filed in support thereof, the Commonwealth's response thereto and a hearing, IT IS HEREBY ORDERED, ADJUDGED AND DECLARED that Defendant's petition is GRANTED based on the attached opinion.

    IT IS FURTHER ORDERED that Defendant's sentence imposed on March 8, 1978, shall be VACATED and a separate Re-Sentencing Scheduling Order will follow.

I didn't add those capital letters, by the way. That's how the form read. My eye caught those big words first—GRANTED ... VACATED! I shouted, "Hallelujah!"

I walked over to my best friend's cell to tell him the news we'd all been waiting for.

"Henry," I said, looking at him through tears in my eyes, my heart pounding. I couldn't speak. He took the Order of the Court out of my hands and read it.

He grabbed me, gave me a big hug, and said, "I knew God heard my prayer for you to go home!"

Soon, everyone heard the good news. The unit went bonkers for me! Guys were cheering. Crying. None of us had ever seen anything like this, or *imagined* anything like this. I just kept thinking about the voice of the Lord—20 months ago, now: "I'll release you!" My heart was pounding. I had to read it over and over—like I might have read it wrong. *Was this...? Did this say...?*

I called and shared the news with my sister. We cried together over the phone. She told me a guy named Jim Neary—though I'd never met him before, he was a friend of a friend of ours—the head of the Probation & Parole, was putting paperwork together for me. She gave me his number so I could call him directly.

"And you know Cindy Harvey from high school," Mary said. "Well, she's Cindy McCarty now, but she works in Jim's office. She's helping, too."

After the call, I was in awe of how God was lining everything up. My friend Cindy from high school was actually working in the probation office of the court house.

Then word came, the date was set—Tuesday, April 3, 2012, at 10:00AM. The place, too: Courtroom 2, Wyoming County Courthouse, Tunkhannock—the very courtroom where I'd been sentenced 34 years earlier.

At some point in March, I called and talked to Jim. He told me that Bill Nast had called and spoken with him a few times, explaining how he and his wife and daughters had been visiting me at Rockview.

"He speaks very highly of you," Jim said. And he added, "Me and Billy have been friends for many years."

He told me, "We are working on many different things at once for you."

One item of importance was getting me a photo ID. "You'll need it to move around," he said.

It hit me: I'd never had a driver's license or photo ID before. Since I was an adult, I'd been AK4192. That's all the ID I'd ever needed.

"I've put your ID committee on that," Jim said.

"Who is my ID committee?" I asked.

"That's Cindy and your sister, Mary."

They were trying to track down my birth certificate and other documentation. It was exciting to know people were going to bat for me—this wasn't idle anymore. *Things were moving.*

When I spoke to Cindy over the phone, she'd say things like, "It's going good, buddy, everything is lining up."

Nobody would give me details—I'm not sure what she could or couldn't say, or if she was guarding against me getting my hopes up. She told me Pastor Larry had sent a letter, letting the court know I had a home plan and a job waiting for me.

There was still a great deal of uncertainty around how things would unfold. My attorney cautioned me, "They're not just going to let you walk out of there a free man. You've spent too many years in prison. There will likely be some transition time and arrangements built in."

It just didn't faze me. Something good was happening. It was no sweat for me to wait a couple of months to see what—I'd be rejoicing all the way!

I was standing in the chow line later, talking with a few friends. I don't remember what we were saying, but I mentioned something about "the perspective of us lifers." There was a strange silence.

My eyes met my friend Jimmy's, and he said, "Not you, Gene! You're not a lifer!" Tears filled my eyes again.

Jimmy was right. It just hadn't dawned on me—I was no longer a lifer.

CHAPTER 14

34 YEARS, 9 MONTHS, AND 15 DAYS

I was practicing with the worship team in the chapel. We were mid-song when two COs walked in. Actually, that in itself was odd—COs didn't come into the chapel. And odder still was that these two guys were not-so-affectionately called "the A-Team," because they were the guys who search and bust inmates and drag them off to the Hole. Needless to say, their entrance captured everyone's attention, and one by one the musicians stalled their playing—like a record slowing ... guitar drops out, bass drops out, percussion drops out. Pretty soon it's just me and my keyboard ... then silence...

"Hello, officers?"

They walked right to me. I guess I expected they might be there to take me away to a holding cell or something, remove me from population. After all, I wasn't a lifer anymore. I was a man imprisoned—for the moment anyway—without a sentence!

They smiled. "We heard the good news," one of them said. And they both reached to shake my hand. Handshakes turned into hugs and pats on the back. It was a surreal moment—for all of us.

I was spending as much time with the guys as possible as April 3rd neared. Warner and I spent time walking the yard, talking about ministry—guys we'd seen into the Kingdom, guys we'd seen growing in their faith. He promised me he would look after some of the men I had invested in over the years.

I tried to avoid talking about my case. Warner prayed for me, asking God to line everything up. Even while he prayed for my case, I knew he had court matters pending of his own—and it wasn't going so smoothly. But Warner had seen a lot of guys leave over the years. He knew God was in control and that we'd all be okay—for tomorrow, too, would be a day the Lord had made!

Henry was my longest and closet friend. We had both avoided talking about the case, dates, and times. It was too emotional. The thought of parting ways after 33 years of friendship was unbearable. While I knew Warner would continue to excel in his walk and service to the Lord, Henry often expressed his deep respect for my walk. I wondered if He'd struggle a bit without me there. I knew the Lord would bless him and keep him, but my heart ached at the thought of not sharing faith's journey as closely with him going forward.

"All the numbers are adding up, Gene," was all Cindy could tell me again on the phone. April 3rd was now just a few days away. They'd be loading me up at Rockview and shipping me to Wyoming County in a few hours. I had no idea what to expect. *Would I be coming back? Would I be going someplace else?*

They had me inventory all my things and move them to R&D.

"If I don't come back, I want to be sure these things get to my friends," I told them.

"Put notes on stuff," they directed. So I did. My TV to this guy; my keyboard to that guy, my books to these guys…

Henry and I were standing in the Dayroom afterward, leaning up against the window talking. I wanted to share with him what God placed on my heart. I told him I knew I was prepared for this moment because I had made relationships a priority over projects.

"Man, that's like a hammer landing a blow on my head, Henry said, looking at me. "I needed to hear that. I get so preoccupied with the projects that I forget people."

I had given him a few large bags of commissary and cosmetic items to hold on to. It was kind of understood that if I didn't come back, he could keep it or pass it out to anyone in need. Henry and I hugged. We both felt the heaviness of the moment. And I was falling apart inside. It felt like I was getting an opportunity that they all deserved, too. But it was just me.

From there, I met the guys in the chapel. Warner and I started reminiscing through all the men we'd met over the years—remembering a lot of the characters, too. We laughed! So much of my life just flowing in memories— "Do you remember that time...?" "Oh my gosh! And that guy...?" "Or that time when...?"

There was no doubt about it—I had so much life to be thankful for! God had blessed me exponentially!

A couple of our guys who'd been out and were back in for parole violations started teasing me about all the changes I'd see on the outside. "They got bluetooths in their ears! They walk around talking out loud, Gene, and you'll be like, 'Who's he talking to?'"

Another guy talked about cars. "Remember a brand-new car in 1977 when you came in? They're antiques now, bro!" Everybody laughed!

We settled down and played some music and sang—my last time with them. I can't really put into words the emotions of that gathering. Guys were ecstatic for me—and at the same time, we all hurt. I hurt. I'd grown up with these guys, spent my life with these guys. They were family. I loved them. While I was very hopeful of being released, that was an overwhelming moment—that I might be moving away from these guys. That they couldn't come with me.

They moved me off the unit before my last night at Rockview—housed me in a transfer cell with the other guys heading out in the morning. My last official act before the trip to court was to return my mattress to the storage room, which brought flashbacks: my arrival at Camp Hill all those years earlier—coming out of isolation and moving into population for the first time, waiting in line to get my mattress out of the storage room and dragging it to my cell. It felt like things had come full-circle. It was a poignant moment.

Then I caught myself—*Careful, Gene. You might just be back here next week dragging this thing out!*

I was trying to be protective of my own emotions. I didn't want to get my hopes up too high, just to be devastated if things didn't work out. *What does "all the numbers are adding up" mean?* Twenty months earlier, I heard the Lord say, "I will release you!" He didn't say when. He didn't say how. He just said "I will," and I needed to trust Him ... and, if necessary, wait on Him even longer.

They put me on a bus to SCI Retreat—ironic name for a jail...

"I'm not going to Dallas?" I asked. That made sense—it was the closest facility to Tunkhannock, and my court appearance.

"Not after what happened to you the last time you were there," they explained. Someone worried my little fall down the stairs wasn't an accident—though I'm certain it was. I guess they'd had some other issues there, and, who knows, with Bobby there, my meeting with him, then the fall—they decided I shouldn't return.

So, sit back and enjoy the ride to Retreat.

The procedure was the same—the Hole. Nothing to occupy your time, but at this point my mind was spinning with anticipation ... what about I didn't even know!

The morning I was to be taken to county, two COs escorted me to the R&D room and had me sit down on a bench.

"Do you know what's happening?" an officer asked.

"I'm headed back to court. Re-sentencing," I said.

He smiled. While he was working on some paperwork, another couple of officers came in.

"Does he know?" one of them asked. More smiles, all around. Then a couple of white-shirts came in, a Captain, a Major, Commissioned Officers, big-wigs.

"What do you hope will happen?" another asked. I muttered something about maybe parole, or a halfway house. Again, lots of smiles.

It was a very weird experience—like they all had more information than I did.

"How much time have you done?" one of the white-shirts asked.

It took me by surprise—I hadn't carried that number in my mind. I went to work on the math. "I was incarcerated at 17. I just turned 52 last month..."

"A long time," the officer short-cut the math for me.

"I guess so," I agreed. But it dawned on me: I was 17 when I came in and I'd spent twice as long on earth as an inmate as I had free.

They dropped a pile of clothing in front of me—sweatpants and a sweatshirt. Not the bright orange jumpsuit I expected. I didn't know what, if anything, to read into it.

"Get dressed," they said. "Sheriffs are here for you."

After changing out of the orange jumpsuit into the clothes they gave me, they turned me over. It was the same in the car for the hour-long ride to county jail: "Are you excited? Do you know what's going to happen?"

Back at County. This trip in was like a blast from the past. I was housed with all these young guys awaiting their hearings or trials.

"You're from Rockview?" guys asked. "What's it like there?" "You were in Camp Hill? Damn! What's that like?" Guys were also nervous. "Will I have to fight there?" "Are there queers there?" "Will guys mess with me?"

My mind ran back through the stories Bobby had told me when I was a kid, all the nerves and fears that danced in my head when I was in these kids' shoes—waiting, wondering, and worrying. Déjà vu.

I gave them the best advice I could: "If you go looking for trouble, you'll find it. Mind your own business … Focus on your education. Your job."

Then I added, "And go to church! That's where the good guys are. Get yourself involved in church!"

Mary came to see me at County the night before my re-sentencing hearing. We met in a visiting room, separated by a little glass partition and speaking on telephone receivers.

"I brought you some clothes," she said. I appreciated it.

I don't' remember saying it, but Mary later recalled that I hadn't wanted to wear them in case they sent me back—I didn't want to have to take off civilian clothes and put back on a prison jumpsuit. In my thinking, the next time I wore civilian clothes, I'd be free.

"Gene, they said the strangest thing to me today," Mary remarked, and her eyes welled up with tears. She was almost whispering on the line. "When I was leaving Jim's office, one of the staffers there asked, 'Mary, does Gene have a ride home tomorrow?' What could that mean?"

It was like lightning to my soul. I started to cry, and to gasp for breath. A war broke out inside me—my emotions wanted desperately to let loose, but, cognitively, I was holding on for dear life.

"No. No. No, don't go there yet!" *I couldn't allow myself to...*

I heard my attorney's words over and over in my head: "You've done so much time, they're not going to just let you out. There will be some transition."

I don't know if I slept that night. I'd been in jail since I was 17, and yet the few hours until 10 the next morning seemed a lifetime! I did opt for the orange prison jumper over the street clothes. I wanted to shave—I looked like a mutt—but they wouldn't give me a razor.

Then came that marvelous shackled walk of shame, back up the middle of the street to the courthouse. *Who would I see today? A jogger? A mom pushing a stroller? Somebody reading the paper on their front porch?*

The deputies escorting me started in with the all-too-familiar question. "Do you know what's going to happen today?"

"I don't know," I said.

"You've got a lot of folks up there in that courtroom," he offered. "A big crowd." He repeated it a few times, too, as we made our way up the street. "Lots of your supporters up there."

I forgot to even notice if any of the neighbors were out as I walked. My mind was spinning a mile a minute over what awaited me.

As we climbed the stairs and came up the hallway into the courtroom, I could sense it was filled to capacity. It was a huge crowd.

I even told myself, *Don't look!* I knew if I did I'd be overcome with emotion. I wanted—needed—to hold myself together.

My heart was pounding so hard I could feel my pulse thumping through my body. I thought my heart might explode! I was trying to calm my breathing, trying to focus. I caught Mary out of the corner of my eye, so I knew where she was. I tried not to see anyone else.

My attorney was talking to me. I'm sure I didn't hear half of what he said. He did repeat his caution to me, that they'd probably want to have me in a program ... something. Whatever. I could feel my pulse in my face, hear it in my ears.

They called the court to session, and the judge came in—covered in a black robe, sitting up on the bench, all authority in his hands. I had a flashback—30-plus years ago, right here, another judge ... and a child. An attorney who didn't say much of anything to me, or for me—a process from which I was completely detached.

It dawned on me that my mother said, years after I was incarcerated, "The judge apologized to me after your sentencing, saying, 'His attorney didn't give the court anything to work with.'"

Back in the moment, now the lawyers were talking. I was missing most of it. The DA said something about me maybe going back to prison a little longer, then applying for parole, and then transitioning into a halfway house. Yep, they'd told me that might happen.

My attorney argued that I'd already served a lot of time. He hoped that the timeline—whatever it included—might be no longer than a year.

A year ... I could do one more year.

While that was going on, Mary shot a look of desperation toward Jim. Jim raised his hand toward her as if to say, "It's okay!" What we didn't know at the time—Jim had written the order that was on the bench, waiting to be signed by the judge. He knew exactly what it said. He smiled at Mary.

There was some more lawyer- and court-speak, back and forth. Once again, what a surreal feeling to have people talking about, even arguing about, your life, your future, and to not be able to weigh in. My next steps were being decided before me—again—and I was a bystander.

Until the judge invited me to speak. "Mr. McGuire," he asked, "do you have anything to say to the court?"

I didn't have anything planned to say, although I'd given some thought to it. I knew I wanted to say "I'm sorry." It was a very emotional moment. The people I'd hurt—the family and friends of Ms. Nagy, the community that knew her and loved her, my sister, Mary, who had to go back to school, her brother and cousin jailed for murder, to grow up in the community bearing that weight ... Dad, Mom, Loren, my brother, Mike—no longer living, but having borne the hurt and burden of it all to their graves ... my friends—the innocence of their teen years shattered by this horrific crime...

I stood.

"Thank you, your Honor. I want to apologize for my crimes. For the victim and to her family, for all the harm I've done—I'm sorry. To my own family, for all the pain I've put them through, and my friends, my high school class, my community—I'm sorry. I also want to say thank you. To everyone here who is helping me today, and to everyone in the system who has cared for me and invested in my life over all these years: Thank you! And thank you, your Honor, for your consideration of my case."

I sat down.

I tell you, in that one moment, a burden of 30-plus years was lifted! This was an opportunity I didn't have when I was 17. It was a brand-new day! *I'm sorry! And, thank you!* In that moment, I was so relieved, the court could have sent me anywhere, for any amount of time—honestly, I was free!

The judge said, "The defendant shall rise." He began to read the order before him:

ORDER OF THE COURT

AND NOW, April 3, 2012, the defendant, Eugene McGuire, is sentenced to pay the costs of prosecution and be committed to the Department of Corrections for confinement in a state institution for a period of not less than 15 years, nor more than 34 years, 9 months and 15 days, and stand committed until complied with.

The defendant shall receive credit for prior confinement in the amount of 34 years, 9 months and 15 days. The defendant has served his maximum sentence imposed and therefore is to be released from confinement, effective this date.

The courtroom exploded! Someone shouted, "Unshackle that man! Release him from those chains! He's a free man!"

I was stunned. I collapsed in tears—sobs of joy, really. People were rushing around. My sister was literally climbing over a rail and a table to reach me.

"Hold on, Mary!" one of the deputies cautioned.

"Out of my way!" she warned. "I've waited 35 years for this, I'm not waiting one more minute!"

I looked up and shouted, "Thank you, your Honor!" He turned and walked quickly out a side door.

I didn't realize it then, but later Jim told me, "He never closed the session; he never dismissed the court." He told me the judge himself was overcome with emotion and chose to step out quickly, with his stenographer left wondering ... *Is it over?* She gathered her materials, with tears in her eyes, and brushed out right behind him.

People have asked me, "What were you thinking when he was reading the order?" And honestly, I was doing math! When he said the maximum sentence was 34 years, nine months, and 15 days, I started trying to figure out, *How close am I?* I wasn't too far from counting on my fingers and toes!

Then when I heard him say, "Released from confinement, effective this day," I fell apart.

God had said, "I'll release you." He had. He did. I never doubted. But I also never imagined...

There were cameras and flashes going off. People were hugging me. My attorney was patting me on the back. The sheriffs, bailiffs—they were rejoicing with us. The celebration was full throttle.

The DA came over to shake my hand.

"Gene," he said, "these two gentlemen would like to meet you." He spun me around and two men, perhaps in their 60s, stood smiling at me.

"These are Isabelle Nagy's nephews." It was as if all the revelry surrounding me fell silent—I heard none of it—and I felt my chest tighten, my mouth go dry.

A million thoughts raced through my head in that instant. I hadn't known any of Ms. Nagy's relatives were there. I couldn't imagine what they'd say to me. Or what I'd say to them. And here we all were, partying—and they'd lost a loved one, after all.

"Congratulations," one of the men said. "Our mother—Aunt Belle's sister—had written a note to the Governor on your behalf years ago. She'd be happy you're out. She thought you'd spent more than enough time in prison."

I thanked them. I said, "I'm so sorry," again. They nodded. Shook my hand.

One at a time, friends lined up to hug me and cry, laugh, and say, "God is awesome, isn't He?!"

Yes, He is! My friend of 25 years, Rob Meier, had driven up from Harrisburg. He stood in tears waiting to hug me.

With the crowd all around me, family, friends, attorney, and sheriffs, I looked up into the gallery and there stood my best friend from high school, Bill Nast. His huge smile expressed everything I was feeling. Time stopped for me in that moment.

I slid through the crowd and climbed up into the gallery. We cried and we hugged. Bill's wife, Karen, and their beautiful daughters, Jordyn and Emily, hugged me next. The hope that they would never have to visit me again in prison—it was a reality!

One of the officers interrupted and said, "Gene, let's get you changed so your sister can take you home!"

He escorted me out the door. We walked back down the block to the jail—still in my orange jumpsuit ... but unshackled, uncuffed. I felt like a brand-new man! I felt like dancing down that street!

When we got to the heavy steel door, the officer buzzed the communication's box and announced, "I am returning Eugene McGuire ... now a free man." We both laughed.

For so many years I'd heard, "I have inmate McGuire here." No more. *Never again.*

While they were gathering the paperwork to process me out, the officer asked that I return to my cell, grab my bedding and mattress, and bring it to the supply closet. More déjà vu. Just as I'd gone to get a mattress and bedding that first night of my incarceration—bookends!

I changed out of that orange jumpsuit and put on jeans and a nice button-down shirt. I couldn't help noticing it wasn't cocoa brown, nor did it have my number, AK4192, stamped on it. The clothes came out of a bag my sister and my friends put together. In it was a bottle of Dolce Gabbana Light Blue cologne, too. I sprayed it once, twice ... *man, it smelled good!*

After the sixth or seventh spray, the officer said, "That's about all you need, Gene! You're gonna have the whole county smelling like cologne!"

Soon I was back facing the large metal locked door, in civilian clothes. I looked through the window and could see the all-out party in the streets waiting for me. I stopped, waiting for the door to buzz. Flashback—all those times of standing and waiting for someone to trigger the lock.

"Gene," a voice said over the speaker, "just push the door. It's open. You're free to go!"

And I was—free to go! As I stepped out, Mary began sprinting toward me, a crowd of my friends and supporters behind her, in pursuit. Hugs. Tears. Shouts of joy. Pictures and video clips of it all exist—I still get teary playing them back now, years later. I cannot even put into words the emotion, the wonder, the awe.

My friend Rob handed me a cell phone. I was aware of cell phones and voicemail—had seen them and heard about them over the years—but they were an entirely new experience to me on April 3, 2012. Back in 1977, talking on the telephone meant you were tethered to a box on a wall, or a table—its only connection a network of wires strung all over the world.

"Leave a message for Pastor Larry," Rob said.

Pastor Larry and Devi couldn't be with us at the courthouse that day because they were ministering in Brazil.

"Larry! Dad! It's me! I'm out! I'm free!" I choked up. "I can't talk," I said, struggling to form words and sentences, fighting sobs of joy. "Everyone is here," I said, looking around and trying to name everyone in the crowd. "Rob is here, and Natalie, and Veronica, and Marty and Marie, and..."

I lost it again emotionally. Tears poured down my cheeks. "This is all the result of you praying for me. I love you! If you're there, pick up! If not, call me. Call me, please! On someone's cell phone. On anyone's cell phone!"

It was late, but I was wide awake. My first night of freedom. It was all still sinking in: I could go anywhere I wanted, do anything I felt like doing. There would be no "lights-out" order coming. No unit, no cell, no bunk—rather the comfortable guestroom bed at my sister's home was turned down and waiting for me. It had been a long and tears-of-joy-filled day. Joe and Mary said goodnight. My niece and nephew turned in, too.

I slid open the glass door and stepped out onto the patio. I sat down in a lawn-chair under the stars. The sights, sounds, and scents of nature enveloped me. It was comfortably cool, and I was wrapped up in a blanket. I sat there all night looking up at the stars—the wonders of His creation spoke hallelujahs! So did my heart!

Freedom ... and the faithfulness of my God ... are very, very good indeed!

CHAPTER 15

GOD GAVE ME THIS STORY SO YOU COULD HEAR IT

I received a life sentence and, along the way, I found life.

I never would have imagined this outcome when, as a 17-year-old high school sophomore, I heard the judge speak those words, "for the rest of your natural life."

Nor when the old-timers laughed at my naivety: "You're a lifer. You're never getting out of here, young buck. You'll die in this prison just like the rest of us lifers."

Nor when I opened the letters over the years, one after another after another, to read, "Application for Commutation DENIED."

Here's the thing: I'm convinced none of it was coincidence.

It wasn't a coincidence that my dad, as fractured as his life and Catholic faith were when I was a young child, desired that I know how to pray the rosary—that he tried to teach me—in hopes that somehow, someday, I'd develop a connection with God.

Nor was it a coincidence that I saw my step-father, Loren, rise early all those mornings and turn through the pages of his old, worn Bible, seeking the face of God before starting each day.

Not a coincidence that a woman I'd never met, in Michigan, received a letter I wrote to my brother in Pennsylvania; that a minster's wife received the note I'd sent to my brother, about getting busted and put in the Hole ... for possession of pot.

Not a coincidence that my mom, who'd spent years languishing at the bottom of a bottle—who I, and everyone who knew her, may rightfully have judged a parental failure—found redemption and recovery in Jesus Christ, and then gave me the very best gift a parent could give: the testimony of a changed life and a renewed heart.

Or that a fellow lifer, a guy called Big Moses, would rise early every morning and sing to God's glory...

Or that a couple of women who worked office jobs at SCI Camp Hill were kind and gracious and demonstrated the love of Jesus Christ to an inmate who happened through their workspace...

Or that Prison Fellowship's Prison Invasion '86 volunteers descended on Camp Hill...

Or that a regular guy was willing to share his own story of alcoholism, a story that hit this inmate right between the eyes...

Or that a pastor spotted this 26-year-old know-it-all-lifer standing alone at Prison Invasion, sensed God's call to "go talk to him," and proceeded to tell me his story, knowing Jesus at 4, sensing a call upon his life at 5...

You've just read my story. You know I could continue—this list could go on for quite some length. But I'll sum it up here: *I believe my story is for you.*

A long time ago, someone a lot smarter than me referred to our God as the Hound of Heaven. It's a strange title, I know. But I've personally experienced the tenacity with which God's love pursues—it's my story ... and it's also yours.

It's not a coincidence that you're holding this book in your hands, or that you've heard my story. God's love is pursuing you, too! I believe He has given me this platform because He wants me to share a few, very specific messages with you.

———————◆———————

God wants me to tell you about forgiveness.

As often as I tell my story, people ask, "Are you angry? Bitter? Are you furious with the system that let you down?"

I understand their questions. Having spent 34 years, nine months, and 15 days in prison for a murder I didn't commit, on what the court later determined to be an unjust sentence, the result of flawed counsel ... do I harbor any unforgiveness in my heart toward those involved?

Or toward my cousin? People tell me, "Bobby led you into this! You were just an impressionable kid, and you didn't know about his crimes, you couldn't see through his deceptions. You didn't know what he was going to do."

I get it. Is my heart hardened toward him? Do I hold him responsible?

Here's what I can tell you: No sin against me has been greater than my sin against God. And as freeing and liberating as it was for me to receive—and know—God's forgiveness in my life, it is every bit as freeing and liberating to forgive and let others go who have hurt me.

God has forgiven all my sins, from participating in a murder, to sexual immorality, to drugs, lying, cheating—it's quite a list! He forgives me and Jesus intercedes on my behalf. The Bible says Jesus acts as my Advocate, like He's seated there at the Father's right hand reminding the Father—even as often as I fail—"He's one of ours! He's your son!"

And my Heavenly Father *is faithful to forgive my sin*, to *remove it as far as the East is from the West*, and to *cleanse me from all unrighteousness*.

Who am I to hold on to an offense? God is quick to forgive me. I need to be quick to forgive others.

The lesson of forgiveness is paramount in my life. It allows me to walk in freedom—without holding grudges. It will do the same for you.

Often when I am asked to speak, I recall the story of the teacher who hit me, even though it had happened before the murder, prison, and all that. It is a memory I held on to for years, with great pain. That experience, as I explained, was like a deep bruise, and whenever something brought it back to my mind, it was like it got poked—it would start aching all over again. All the embarrassment, all the shame, rushed back. And I hated that man all over again. I wanted him to hurt the way I'd hurt. I wanted him to get his—as if that would somehow heal *my* heart. Of course, it wouldn't. And here's the really pathetic part of it...

My holding on to it, my unforgiveness, bitterness, and anger, wasn't affecting him in the least. It was affecting me! I was suffering ... still!

Forgiving those who've hurt you is hard. In Matthew 18, Peter comes to Jesus and asks, "How many times shall I forgive my brother or sister who has sinned against me? Seven times?"

Think about that question. Do you suppose Peter might have had someone particular in mind? Maybe someone had hurt him, then denied it, like my teacher. Or perhaps they had offered up a disingenuous apology, a flippant *I'm sorry*, only to repeat the offense.

Maybe that's why Peter asked, "How many times, Lord? Seven times?"

Jesus answered, in essence, "Get out your calculator! Let's do some math!" A paraphrase, of course.

Bible scholars suggest Christ's answer, his formula of "seventy times seven," is really a way of saying "forgive an infinite or perfect number of times."

And Jesus makes it clear that is His intention—He uses a story to illustrate.

There was a king who decided to settle accounts with his servants. One servant was brought in who owed the king more money than he could ever hope to pay off. He fell to his knees and begged for mercy. The king mercifully and graciously forgave the man's debt.

In the very next scene of the story, that freshly forgiven servant went out and found a man who owed him a small amount of money by comparison. The debtor begged for forgiveness. The servant began to choke the man, demanding repayment. When the man couldn't repay the amount, the servant had him thrown into a debtor's jail.

The king, then, hearing of the unmerciful servant's behavior, called him back in and asked, "Shouldn't you have had mercy on your fellow servant just as I had on you?" The king handed him over to the jailers—don't miss this—"to be tortured."

Unforgiveness tortures you. It locks you up and torments your heart. When you hold tightly to these things, you're the one paying the price. You're the one losing sleep—like sleeping with a wet dog: it's miserable, it stinks. Why are you doing it? Put that dog out of the bed! Get a set of fresh, sweet-smelling linens! Get a good night's sleep!

People do ask, "Are you angry? Are you bitter?" When I tell them I'm not, I've seen God use it powerfully in their lives.

I was in Oklahoma, not long after I'd been released from prison. I was working for Pastor Larry's son-in-law, James, a roofing contractor. As James and his team were fixing roofs, God bumped me into a number of people and gave me opportunities to share my testimony. One day we stopped at a supplier's office. James went in only to emerge a few minutes later, calling, "Gene! Come in here!"

James introduced me to Big John—a large man who sat behind a large desk. "Gene, tell him your story," James urged.

I gave a condensed version. Before I finished, I noticed Big John wiping tears from his eyes. I looked over and saw James was, too. It was contagious— next thing I knew, I was wiping away my own. God was at work here.

"My sister was killed several years ago," Big John opened up. "Gene, I've held on to anger, resentment, bitterness, for all these years. God has used your story to show me I need to let it go."

I had no idea of Big John's background as I shared. I was just giving my testimony. But the Holy Spirit uses our stories to reveal Himself to others.

I saw Big John several times after that day. You could actually see the fruit of the work God was doing in his heart. His countenance, his joy— even his physical appearance—changed before my eyes. It looked like someone removed a heavy weight from around his neck. Now he could live, unencumbered. And so can you.

Another instance: I was invited to lunch by a friend, Kim. She wanted to introduce me to a couple she knew. The wife began with the usual: "So, Gene, where are you from?" Which led to, "What did you do in Pennsylvania?"

I glanced over to Kim, and she was wearing a Cheshire Cat grin, as if to say, "Oh, I can't wait to hear this!"

And it's at this point in interactions that people expect you to tell them about your career field, or education, or hobbies, or associations. I can promise you, nobody is anticipating, "Actually, I was doing life ... for murder." It tends to produce a jaw-dropping effect.

Once that revelation was out of the bag, the wife was really intrigued and wanted the full story. I obliged. Her husband didn't seem as interested. He was polite in listening, but never spoke up. When we finished lunch, we exchanged all the usual pleasantries, "Nice to have met you," and so on. That was that.

A couple months later, I was at a dinner engagement ... and who walks in? This couple. Our eyes met, and the husband rushed to greet me.

"Gene! It's so great to see you!" He couldn't wait to tell me his story. "A few years back, I was the CEO of a company, and the Board made an unexpected decision to let me go. I was devastated," he said. "And the timing couldn't have been worse—we'd just begun construction on a new home. We lost everything. But your story—God used what you shared that day at lunch to show me I'd been holding on to hurt, refusing to forgive ... I was trapped. Gene, God spoke to my heart. He told me to let it go. I did. He set me free!"

The man's wife echoed his joy and added that, through this, God brought healing they'd never imagined into their hearts, their marriage, and home. This is our God.

Let me be clear: This is *your* God! He forgives you. And He will give you the grace you need to forgive others—to experience healing, relief, and joy! *To live!*

The next lesson I believe God wants me to share with you is that everybody gets off-track at some point in life's journey. Everyone is going to slip up from time to time. That is why it is so important that you be teachable and correctable.

As a young man, I knew it all. You know what I mean? Can you relate? When people tried to speak into my life, my pat answer was, "I know!" If I'm really honest, looking back, I acted as if I knew everything to mask my insecurities.

And let me tell you, prisons are full of guys who know it all! You've never seen such a collection of smart guys as populate cell blocks! Brilliance!

It recently dawned on me—the irony—the prison system is called "The Department of Corrections," and those who serve there are called "Corrections Officers," and they run "Correction Facilities." You'd think the smart guys go to Harvard, but the real smart ones, the ones who know it all ... they go to Corrections!

Guys who insist they know it all—you know people like this—their lives become unmitigated disasters. They get off-track and lack the sense to realize it, the courage to admit it, and the humility to be taught or corrected. I've learned so many life lessons from Pastor Larry Titus over the years. Perhaps none as crucial as this—being teachable and correctable ensures that, when you fall, you'll get back on.

Proverbs is full of wisdom on this subject. Sayings like *Whoever remains stiff-necked after many rebukes will suddenly be destroyed—without remedy.* And, *Whoever disregards discipline comes to poverty and shame, but whoever heeds correction is honored.*

Don't miss this rich promise found in Scripture: *If any of you lacks wisdom, you should ask God, who gives generously to all without finding fault, and it will be given to you.*

Crave wisdom. Become willing to learn from anybody, and in every circumstance. You'll grow for it! It doesn't have to be a preacher with a pulpit or a teacher with tenure. God uses everyone and everything. In fact, He often uses the foolish and lowly to get our attention. A Christian brother or sister might be God's chosen vessel to reach you. He could use an unbeliever to teach you. He might even use an enemy to correct you. In the Bible, God once spoke a corrective lesson through the mouth of an ass! I'm not kidding—look it up! Numbers 22. He loves you that much—He will get the message through to you. The question is, *Will you heed it?*

Humble yourself. Become a student of Jesus. The process is called discipleship—become a disciple, a learner, a follower. Grow.

Methetes is the Greek word translated *disciple* in English. It means "one who willingly sits under another in order to learn." It would be ridiculous to approach your teacher the first day of the semester with the mindset that "I can't learn anything here; I already know all that he or she can teach me." A decision needs to be made to submit. Are you here to learn? To be corrected?

My commitment to become a disciple of Jesus Christ followed naturally after I accepted Him as Lord and Savior. It came from the overwhelming love I experienced for Him, a response to His love for me. When I read the gospels and saw the way He invested His life into His disciples, training them to go on and change the world—and when I witnessed Pastor Larry emulate Christ, investing of himself in me—I knew this was who God intended me to be.

You see, being a disciple is about more than showing up at church on Sunday, raising your hands, and singing praises. It means surrendering your life—every aspect and avenue of your life—to the authority of Jesus Christ, and those chosen instruments of instruction, correction, and training He sees fit to send into your world.

· ————⟫•⟪———— ·

That leads me to the third lesson I believe God wants me to share with you—the importance of the process. I hope my story lends credibility and authenticity to my telling you that the process is in God's hands, for as long as it takes and to whatever lengths or depths it travels.

All the dots connect. The faintest glimpses of light when I walked in abject darkness ... the lessons I refused to hear and had to learn dragging my feet, kicking and screaming ... the places where I was surprised ... the places where I was dumbstruck ... the places where I was forced to my knees without the strength or the courage to bear the weight...

One thread ran consistently through it all and tied—and continues to tie—it together: God.

In Christendom, so much weight is placed on calling and anointing. "Who God calls, He also anoints," preachers say.

That's true, but let me tell you what the Word of God says. It promises that when God calls you, He will *equip you with everything good for doing his will, and may he work in us what is pleasing to him.* That, my friends, is a process!

And that is something I believe God wants you, reading this book, to hear: The process is vitally important!

As you might imagine, another immensely popular question people ask me after so many years incarcerated is, "Are you looking for a wife?"

I will say: the thought may have crossed my mind. It is actually a great place for me to illustrate—and apply—the importance of this lesson.

After so many years separated from women, and believing that God has the very best gifts and blessings in mind and in store for me, every time I see a pretty girl, carrying a Bible, look my way, I could think, "There she is! It's a sign from God!"

The Bible teaches us to wait upon the Lord. We humans don't do waiting well. I've felt the pain of crashing through the guardrails of His Word designed to protect us. Relationships that begin without God's approval can end with people getting hurt.

Today I'm really trying to embrace God's process and trust Him for the timing where my dating life is concerned. Remember what I said about the process sometimes feeling long, though? Take it from me ... it can feel very long.

When I think of the importance—and the difficulty—of God's process running its course in our lives, a couple of Bible stories stand out.

Consider Joseph's story in the book of Genesis. He was 17 when he had a dream—God revealed a calling upon his life to rule even over his brothers.

Seventeen! You know the story—but do revisit it in Genesis 37-50.

Joseph's jealous brothers sold him into slavery. Through twists and turns over time, he rose to a place of prominence in Egypt. Then, he was falsely accused and thrown into prison. By the way, don't miss the fact that Scripture records, *God was with Joseph while he was in prison.* God never leaves nor forsakes you. This is a reality. I can add a hearty "Amen!"

The story continues: Joseph grew in favor in the eyes of the warden and was given responsibility within the prison.

Next he had an encounter with Pharaoh's cup-bearer in jail and interpreted dreams for him. In return, Joseph requested, *When you find favor in Pharaoh's eyes, remember me; mention me.* The cup-bearer said he would.

Yet the chapter ends with Joseph, forgotten. Can you feel the pain of it? No? How about the first words of the very next chapter? It begins, *When two full years had passed...*

Two more years!

Those two additional years were necessary. God was accomplishing more in Joseph's heart, and in others', and aligning other facets of the bigger picture. Joseph didn't—and we don't often in our own lives—get an explanation of just why the delay was necessary. What was happening behind the scenes? God doesn't consult us. He's God. We're not. And that's big: God has impressed that truth on me again and again in my process.

It happened once while I prepared for my fourth attempt at filing for commutation. I was so very hopeful that this time, at long last, all the pieces were aligned. I had spent weeks working on my file, gathering all the materials needed, dotting every "i" and crossing every "t." It was so time-consuming, in fact, that I took my entire file—all the documentation—with me to my desk in the storeroom so I could work on it during any spare moment I had.

An inmate at the time from our housing unit manipulated a female staff member into sneaking a cell phone in for him. They got busted, and security launched a thorough investigation of the entire institution. On my unit, the Honor Block, they removed all the long-term offenders, placing us in segregation for three days.

When things finally returned to normal, I filed my paperwork. After I did, I learned a new Lieutenant of Security had been appointed. I was concerned—in the past I'd had a strong recommendation from the Security Department. But a new head of security wouldn't know me and couldn't, therefore, make a recommendation. This was reason for legitimate concern.

The day of my hearing came. I sat down—everything was going along great. Then it came time for the new Lieutenant to speak. He began just as I had feared.

"I'd been reluctant to vote on this inmate," he said, "because I'm unfamiliar with him." But then he went on to explain circumstances that left me amazed—and reminded me, undoubtedly, that God holds the process in His capable hands.

During our lockdown over the cell phone incident, security searched the storeroom office where I worked. Noticing the stack of paperwork to the side of my desk, officers brought it to the Lieutenant. He looked through it personally. It was my file, past to present, top to bottom, inside and out, delivered directly to the one man who needed to get to know me before this hearing.

After he read my paperwork, he had officers return it. I was no wiser that it had ever been disturbed.

"I vote an enthusiastic 'yes' on Gene's application," he concluded. The team then voted unanimously in favor of my release to the Board of Pardons. That window of delay—the inconvenience of it—was a divine appointment.

I was eventually denied by the Board of Pardons again—that political juggernaut I've mentioned before. But I cannot tell you how encouraged I was to know the Lord had worked behind the scenes, moving people into the right places at just the right times, providing another glimpse of His sovereignty over me.

So ... back to Joseph.

In time, the cup-bearer remembered him before Pharaoh. Joseph rose again in prominence in Egypt. He was put in authority over everything in Pharaoh's realm. Process. Process. More process. And then famine set in.

Joseph was in charge of the supply of grain, and who arrived desperately in need of food? His brothers! Some 20-plus years of process laid the groundwork for this moment. All the pieces were aligned, perfectly, by the hand of God.

God's glory is truly revealed, when, at the end of his story, Joseph says to his brothers, *You intended to harm me, but God intended it for good to accomplish what is now being done, the saving of many lives.*

Another example is from the life of King David. God sent Samuel to call and anoint David king over Israel. David, you remember, was a teenage shepherd boy at the time. Called, anointed ... and let the years-long process toward his coronation begin.

Oh, and what a painful season it was! David must have wondered at any number of junctures along the way, "God? Are you seeing what's happening? Are you still in this?"

Having the vantage point that we do now, as with Joseph's story, we're able to look back over the entirety of David's plight and see the big picture—the end that contextualizes the means. But as he went through those experiences, it had to be a real head-scratcher. We can see now that each step of the way was prelude to what would follow—it all rolled into making a king, and, even more than that ... maturing David into *a man after God's own heart.*

The process for me began when God foreknew me, chose me, and predestined me to be conformed into His image. It began, the Bible says, before time. It declares me to be His workmanship—literally His work of art—with specific works He created for me to do. The same is true of you.

From before my first breath, through my adolescence and those daring beach escapes from Sunday School, through my high school experience and the ill-conceived date with the Christian girl (to a movie theatre, NOT the drive-in), through conviction and sentence, through 34 years, nine months, and 15 days...

Even the process between God's "I will release you" to the day I walked out, unshackled, was years-long. Every step of the process took longer than it seemed it should.

I remember when my new attorney called me for the very first time, that's what he said: "Gene, this is going to take some time." And that first hearing date they'd set for me had to be delayed. And then the second. And the third. They call it a continuance, by the way, when a court proceeding is delayed. *Continuance*—the wait continues.

But time wasn't passing indiscriminately or idly. When I waited, for weeks on end, for a bus to return me from SCI Dallas to Rockview ... I hated every moment, feeling like I'd been forgotten by the system, perhaps even by God, wondering—*What in the world is happening? What am I still doing here?* Then came that out-of-nowhere encounter with my cousin. Had I been moved out in what I deemed a timelier manner, that visit never would have happened.

You see, God's got this. God's got you. God's in the process.

Here's my bottom line: God is so extravagant in His love, He will absolutely mess with your life to bring about His end—your best, and the very best for others.

Allow me to give you one more example of the extravagance of God's love—His pursuing, His process.

Do you remember the story in the Bible where Jesus and His disciples set out to cross a lake in a boat and a storm arose? And Jesus calmed the storm? Do you remember where they were headed?

If you read the passage, you'll see, they landed on a shore where Jesus met—and healed and delivered—a man oppressed by a legion of demons. That man was set free! Talk about unshackled. Jesus cast the demons, you may recall, into a herd of pigs, which promptly ran off a cliff. (That's when Jesus invented "Deviled Ham" ... and now you know: I have no future in comedy!)

But you might have missed one little point in the story. After freeing that one man, Jesus and His disciples got back in the boat and sailed away. In other words, they went on a time-consuming, costly, dangerous cruise that day to meet the needs of just one soul in peril!

That's the extravagance of God's love!

So rejoice! If God decides you're to minister to one soul stranded on a deserted island, I tell you, He may just allow your ship to sink and sustain you for a week floating on driftwood just to get you there. Ask the apostle Paul—shipwrecked, jailed, beaten, dragged out of towns, his life in jeopardy. Process.

We're all in process. And we will be until the day we go home to Jesus— that's when the process is complete. Situations, circumstances, and even entire seasons within the process can be extremely trying. When they are, rejoice! These are the things that get you from where you've been to where you're going. God is in this! And you'd be foolish to try to short-change His process.

At certain points of your journey, you might be able to look back and see some of it. Things that at the time made zero sense to you may, one day, become a little clearer. I can do that, now. Looking back at the transport delays that let me see Bobby, the cell-phone incident that allowed the new Lieutenant to discover my file ... it's a real blessing when you can say, "Oh! That's what it was all about!" But other pieces of the puzzle you'll likely be left to wonder about this side of heaven. You simply have to trust.

How would my life have unfolded if I hadn't gone out to play pool with Bobby that night? If I hadn't been convicted of second-degree murder? If I hadn't been sentenced to life without the possibility of parole? If I hadn't spent 34 years, nine months, and 15 days behind bars?

Here's what I can tell you—all those things are a part of who I am today. And I'm thankful!

I've been asked if I have any regrets. Sure, there are things I wish I could undo, or do over. But you can't change the past. Someone once pointed out that when you're in the driver's seat, the view offered by the rearview mirror is so very small compared to the expansive view looking forward, through the windshield. It's so true.

You can make a decision to live in the present, in this moment. And realize this: What you do today—in the present—can affect tomorrow. In fact, what you do today can have an eternal impact! You don't live in the past. Believe that your future is ahead of you, and, by all means, remove that rearview mirror from your life! Live in the present!

Pastor Larry reminded me of Romans 8:28 often. Usually, as I recall, it was on the heels of hard days or difficult circumstances. *And we know that in all things God works for the good of those who love him, who have been called according to his purpose.*

He'd always emphasize the word ALL. "All things"—the good, the bad, the ugly. I admit, when I was in the middle of a discouraging experience, these words were about the last thing I wanted to hear. But they're so true. I know it—I'm living proof.

Were there moments when I doubted? When I was afraid? When I was depressed or discouraged? Absolutely! There were times when I was like the prophet Jonah, sitting under a wilting shade tree, whining! But those are honest moments before God—the kind of on-your-knees-vulnerable moments that are healthy and ripe and important for learning and course correction.

She wasn't a prophet of God, but little orphan Annie was speaking Gospel truth when she said, "The sun'll come out tomorrow." With God, it's absolutely the case! He's accomplishing something in your life. He will be faithful to finish the good work He's started in you—guaranteed! I want to be found faithful. I want to be found trusting Him, walking in Him, waiting upon Him. How about you?

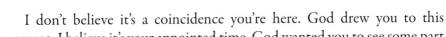

I don't believe it's a coincidence you're here. God drew you to this moment. I believe it's your appointed time. God wanted you to see some part of my story to reveal His love for you! And I trust Him—He knows what part of my story connects with you and yours. In fact, I'm always amazed how with different people it's different things.

No matter where you are today, I assure you, God has not forgotten you, He's not abandoned you, He's not aloof to your hurts. He's heard your cries. He's been close—preventing your suffering from extending beyond His perfect purpose. God is as close to you right now as He was to His Son Jesus when He died on the cross, where He knew such suffering would lead to the salvation of many!

The wounds caused by another, the neglect and abandonment of loved ones and friends, the offenses of business partners or employers, the shortcomings, disappointments, and even sins of ministers and Christian friends—whomever, whatever, however ... God has never allowed so much as an ounce of it to go wasted in your life. He's been growing and preparing you.

Turn to Jesus. Cling to Jesus. The best is yet to come!

Thank You for Reading

Thank you for taking the time to read *Unshackled: From Ruin to Redemption.* I hope you've enjoyed reading my story as much as I've enjoyed sharing it.

Gene McGuire

Gene McGuire is an in-demand speaker, sharing his testimony and teaching on matters of faith. For information on scheduling him for your church, conference, or event, contact him through his website **www.genemcguire.org** or by email at **speak@genemcguire.org**

For additional copies of *Unshackled: From Ruin to Redemption* email **books@genemcguire.org**

Connect with Gene via Social Media thru www.genemcguire.org

Gene McGuire
P.O. Box 1041
Colleyville, TX 76032